THE MYTH *of*
OVERPUNISHMENT

The MYTH *of* OVERPUNISHMENT

FIRST EDITION

Copyright 2022 Barry Latzer

ISBN: 9781645720324 (Hardcover)

ISBN: 9781645720331 (ebook)

For inquiries about volume orders, please contact:

Republic Book Publishers

27 West 20th Street

Suite 1103

New York, NY 10011

editor@republicbookpublishers.com

Published in the United States by Republic Book Publishers

Distributed by Independent Publishers Group

www.ipgbook.com

Book designed by Mark Karis

Printed in the United States of America

BARRY LATZER, JD, PHD

THE MYTH *of*
OVERPUNISHMENT

A DEFENSE *of the* AMERICAN JUSTICE SYSTEM

and a PROPOSAL *to* REDUCE INCARCERATION

WHILE PROTECTING *the* PUBLIC

REPUBLIC

BOOK PUBLISHERS

CONTENTS

FOREWORD

BY SENATOR TOM COTTON

BY ANY INFORMED MEASURE, the criminal justice system in the United States is extraordinarily lenient. In fact, it is more lenient than at any point in our history. This is true if measured by the number of criminals who face consequences for their crimes through arrests and convictions, but also if measured by the consequences that we impose. Many readers may be surprised by that fact, especially if they have consumed much of the fashionable—if ill-backed—talking points that are popular among decarcerationists and soft-on-crime advocates today.

Virtually everyone in the United States knows someone whose life has been touched by crime. Some have experienced serious crime, or have even lost a loved one to senseless violence, while others have experienced the violating feeling of being victimized by petty theft or vandalism. A substantial number of Americans have also been connected, whether directly or indirectly, with someone who has been arrested for a crime at some level. Yet despite the commonality of personal experience, the rhetoric surrounding criminal justice policy is not only heated but often mostly devoid of fact. So, when I was asked to write a foreword for a new book by Dr. Barry Latzer, one of America's preeminent criminologists and an expert with a knack for cutting through the fact-free vitriol on this topic, I was intrigued.

According to popular belief, the United States locks up vast numbers of people for minor crimes or "low-level" offenses, such as minor drug possession or mere "administrative" infractions, and those offenders are subjected to severe sentences that are decades longer than necessary. Advocates of this view attach scary labels like "mass incarceration," as if swaths of people are being indiscriminately rounded up and herded into prisons in scenes reminiscent of concentration camps. The result, allegedly, is that our criminal justice system wastes shocking amounts of money on lengthy sentences for minor offenders, and that those offenders only become more crime-prone as a result of their unjust incarceration. Such talking points are typically followed by proposals for "reform" that purport to focus the justice system on violent and "serious" criminals by drastically reducing enforcement of other offenses. It would be a compelling argument, if only it weren't based entirely on fiction.

There is a group of activists that has taken this false narrative a step further, arguing that the justice system hasn't expanded to inadvertently ensnare small-time offenders, but that the system itself was designed as a tool of oppression from the beginning. According to this theory, the very existence of criminal punishment in the United States has never been anything other than institutionalized racism, bigotry, and class-based hatred, used by the rich and powerful to keep everyone else down. This, too, is nothing but fiction.

The truth, as Dr. Latzer makes clear, is that in the United States, "low-level" offenders don't go to prison for any significant length of time. Typically, such offenders don't go to prison at all, instead receiving slap-on-the-wrist consequences like fines, community service, or probation. The drug offenders who see more than nominal prison time are incarcerated for drug trafficking offenses, not "low-level" simple possession offenses, and even they do not drive our overall incarceration rates. Criminal justice defendants are not systemically targeted for their race or affinity group, either. And the vast majority of offenders with lengthy prison terms are behind bars for violent offenses, especially murder, aggravated assault, and rape.

What, then, of the point that the United States has such high incarceration rates? It's true that the United States in the last several decades has reached historically-high prison population numbers—both in terms of absolute numbers and per-capita rates. But those who claim that this proves their theory of overincarceration are able to see only one small part of the picture.

In the last half-century, crime rates skyrocketed as criminal leniency views reigned supreme, peaking in the 1990s before the public awakened and demanded stronger law enforcement. Taking back American streets and communities from unfettered violence naturally resulted in more convictions, and inmate numbers swelled. Technology, including everything from security cameras to ballistics and nationwide, searchable databases, has also made it easier to solve crimes than at any point in the past.

Despite improvements in and emphasis on law enforcement, the vast majority of crimes in the United States never result in so much as an arrest, much less a conviction or prison sentence. Less than half of reported violent crimes in the United States ever result in arrest. This is true even for murder (undoubtedly the most serious criminal offense), as four out of every ten homicides are never cleared.

The numbers are worse for rape and robbery, where two-thirds of offenders aren't caught. And more than 80 percent of property crimes are never solved, either. Those who focus on comparing incarceration rates in the United States to incarceration rates elsewhere—or to incarceration rates of the United States in decades and centuries past—miss one simple point: The "right" number of inmates should be determined by how many people commit crimes. And by that metric, the United States has a serious under-incarceration problem.

What Dr. Latzer has done in this book is to administer a much-needed dose of reality to the criminal justice debate. Dr. Latzer's chronicling of the history and development of punishment in America makes plain that our methods of administering criminal penalties today are humane, transparent, and consistent by any historical measure. The inherent fairness that accompanies certainty and consistency is obvious in the context of past justice systems that had neither. And anyone who peddles the lie that our criminal justice system is merely a tool of oppression needs only to review this history to understand that, although there have been many systems used to oppress and marginalize various groups throughout antiquity, the modern criminal justice system in America isn't one of them.

One of the most exciting aspects of this book is that it does not settle for defending the American criminal justice system in the context of history alone, nor does it take the easy route frequented by soft-on-crime and tough-on-crime advocates alike of merely calling for more or less law enforcement. Instead, it offers a glimpse at the possible criminal justice system of the future.

An argument often marshalled by decarcerationists is that the criminal justice system is too costly. While the costs of the criminal justice system pale in comparison to the costs of unfettered crime, it is true that transparent due process and safe, secure incarceration and post-release monitoring are an expensive investment. Dr. Latzer's thoughts on the future of electronic monitoring—or "e-carceration"—offer a vision of how technology can reduce these costs and increase efficiency.

As this book makes clear, the concept of punishment has constantly evolved in the American saga, and our attention to that evolution can ensure that we improve justice itself without falling prey to the folly and failure of leniency.

—SENATOR TOM COTTON

INTRODUCTION

THIS BOOK IS A RESPONSE TO A MYTH, the myth of "mass incarceration." Google the term and you will get almost half a million results. Everyone talks about it: professors, criminal justice experts, journalists, and so on. But what exactly does "mass incarceration" mean? And why do I call it a "myth"?

The term refers to the number of offenders who are in jail or prison in the United States, which we can round off to 2.2 million.[1] The implication is that this number is too high, that the United States must be overpunishing people. That's the myth.

If we were overpunishing, it would be because of two different practices, or some combination of both. Either too many people are being jailed or imprisoned, or too many prisoners are serving unjustifiably long sentences. In part 2 of this book, I'll fully explain why neither is occurring. But just to give you a foretaste, I briefly address these claims, starting with the allegation that too many people are incarcerated.

The first thing that tells you this overpunishment claim is dubious is that there are millions of crimes in the United States each year, many more than the number of offenders in jails and prisons. So lots of criminals are not being punished at all, or they've been given wrist-slap sentences, such as probation, which means no imprisonment whatsoever. In fact, 31 percent of all convicted felons and 23 percent of violent offenders are released without spending a single day in prison![2]

Consider these undisputed numbers: Crime survey victims reported the equivalent of 5.8 million violent attacks and 12.8 million property crimes (such as burglary) in 2019 alone, for a total of 18.6 million criminal victimizations.[3] Forty-four percent of these crimes (8.1 million) were reported or otherwise known to the police, who then made over 10 million arrests.[4] The overwhelming majority of the 10 million people arrested did not go to prison and probably didn't spend much time in jail either. There were 1.43 million jail admissions in 2018/19 and 577,000 prison entries in 2019.[5] Even if we account for the imperfect syncing of the numbers—the admitted prisoners may have committed their crimes in previous years—it should be obvious that the number of crimes far outstrips the number incarcerated.

Sure, the issue is more complicated than I'm acknowledging at this point. But I hope I've at least planted a seed of doubt in your mind. Just remember: 18.6 million victimizations a year and 2.2 million incarcerated.

Then there's the other piece of the overpunishment issue: the contention that we punish prisoners too severely. To analyze this claim, it is useful to compare present-day practices to our past. Part 1 presents a brief history of punishment in the United States. A lot of that history is ugly, even stomach-churning. It will probably make you angry. But the history shows one thing clearly: today's prisoners are treated better than at any other point in American history. The punishments we impose today are less harsh, less racist, and more lenient than they ever have been. By historical standards there is no case for overpunishment.

Another measure of our alleged severity is the relatively lenient treatment of prisoners in other countries, especially in Europe and among such English-speaking nations as Canada and Australia. I concede that our punishments are indeed harsher than those of other countries: American prisoners generally serve more time behind bars. Though the decarcerationists eagerly point this out, they don't discuss the reasons for the difference, and there are some compelling explanations. For instance, gun crimes, virtually unknown in Europe, generate much longer sentences in the United States. Recidivism is another factor: repeaters get lengthier sentences, and we have many more repeat offenders than the comparable countries. In any event, despite our relatively high incarceration rates, American prisoners don't spend a great deal of time behind bars: two-thirds of the offenders released from state prison in 2018 had served less than two years.[6] So we're not nearly as mean or irrational as the decarcerationists claim.

I'll address the above issue in more detail in part 2, where I'll also speak to the contention that African Americans are being singled out for unfair punishment. That, too, is a myth. Though people of color are disproportionately incarcerated, this is due to their high crime rates, especially for violent crimes, not racial discrimination.

In short, the claim that the United States overpunishes is dubious. Despite this, the movement to reduce incarceration is powerful nowadays, maybe inexorable. To make matters worse, the reformers offer no workable alternative, no acceptable plan for downsizing. Their proposals, whether "bail reform" on the front end or "deprisonization" on the back end, would free dangerous people. Some of these released offenders are violent; many are recidivists. Guess who will pay the price for such policies? We need to find a way to reduce incarceration (if we must) without increasing public risk.

Fortunately, we have other options. At the end of the book, I'll explain why dramatically expanding our electronic monitoring capacity is a much better idea than schemes to release dangerous offenders. Instead of decarcerating we should be e-carcerating. Electronic surveillance systems will help keep offenders from violating the terms of their release and being sent (or returned) to prison. Surveillance will also enable safe bail reform, by substituting electronic monitoring for money bail, which now leads to the jailing of thousands of low-income arrestees who have not yet been convicted of any crime. Through the use of already available technology, we can so closely monitor pretrial defendants, probationers, and parolees that the need for jail and prison will likely decline. E-carceration, in short, can reduce traditional incarceration, thereby saving money on expensive lock-ups, help offenders reform and reintegrate into law-abiding society, and protect the public. It's win-win-win.

If Americans are serious about reducing incarceration, we should launch an e-carceration campaign. As our technological capacities improve, we may even reach a point where the United States can radically decarcerate and replace much of its incarceration with e-carceration. We aren't anywhere near that point yet, and we're unlikely to get there for some time. In the interim we will still need our prisons, and despite the naysayers, they do a reasonable job of justice for all.

***

Now I will briefly review the fascinating history of punishment in the United States and you'll see why I say that in light of past conditions, the contemporary prisoner has very little to complain about. By historical measures overpunishment is most certainly a myth.

PART ONE

A SHORT HISTORY OF
PUNISHMENT IN AMERICA

1

MAIM AND SHAME: COLONIAL-ERA PUNISHMENTS

EVERYONE'S HEARD of the Salem (Massachusetts) witch hunts, which led to twenty executions in a single year (1692), in a town with a population of only two thousand. ("Witch hunt," referring to an unwarranted investigation, has become a common expression among English speakers—even United States presidents.) Salem involved a moral panic, so in many ways it was not at all typical of colonial justice. But it does teach us some things about the colonial era, which ran from 1607 to 1776. In the New England colonies, controlled by Puritans, religion was the main driver of criminal law. To the Puritans there was little difference between crimes and moral transgressions: crimes were sins and sins were crimes.

Profaning the Sabbath, for instance, could get one whipped. One book on crime in early New England lists the following cases of Sabbath desecration, a mere handful of the many hundreds of such prosecutions.[1]

- In 1630, in Boston, John Baker was whipped "for shooting at fowle on the Sabbath day."

- Humfry Griffin was convicted for unloading barley before the sun set on Sunday.

- In 1670, John Lewis and Sarah Chapman were presented at Connecticut Colony Court "for sitting together beneath the apple tree on the Lord's Day."

- In 1647, the Wenham, Massachusetts, constable was called before the Essex County Court for delivering a prisoner to Salem on the Lord's Day.

- Captain Kemble spent several hours locked in the Boston stocks in 1656 "for lewd and unseemly behavior on the Sabbath." Returning home after three years at sea, Captain Kemble had kissed his wife!

We may smirk at this last example, but the stocks (wooden beams with carve-outs locked around the head, legs, and arms of the seated miscreant) were no laughing matter. Pillories, which required the transgressor to stand while head and hands protruded from openings in the wood, were even more uncomfortable. Both exposed one to taunts and jeers, to say nothing of a pelting with trash, rotten eggs, and mud by local boys.

It could be worse: New Hampshire law gave the courts discretion to impose the pillory, whipping, boring of the tongue with a red-hot iron, or standing on the gallows with a rope on one's neck for "Denying, Cursing, or Reproaching the Holy Word of God."[2]

A second takeaway from Salem is that public hangings were common in colonial America, at least for the crimes that the establishment considered the most atrocious. In fact, nearly *all* punishments (fines an obvious exception) were public. The colonial authorities wanted offenders to be shamed and humiliated before their friends and neighbors. The idea was to deter them along with the townsfolk who could see and empathize with their distress.

For a time this worked. Colonial America was small-town America. Even as late as 1760, only seven colonial cities had more than three thousand people, and in 1775, on the eve of the American Revolution, Philadelphia, the biggest city, had only twenty-three thousand.[3] Where everyone knew everyone else, the embarrassment of public punishment was all the more acute.

There were no prisons as we know them in colonial America. A prison is designed to house offenders, to cut them off from society for a fairly long time, the length of the sentence depending on the reprehensibility of the crime and past misdeeds. Colonials didn't have such a concept and wouldn't have been able to pay for a prison if they had.[4]

The colonies did have jails—little more than houses with four or five rooms—intended to hold people awaiting trial (as does the modern-day jail). They also confined debtors, including those sentenced to compensate crime victims (restitution) but who never paid up. Jails stank and in summer were broiling hot. They didn't even segregate males and females. But inmates could, in some colonies, walk out, provided they remained within the jail "bounds," and returned at night to sleep.[5] These were the colonial version of today's halfway houses.

Since there were no prisons, what punishments did the colonists impose? The answer is execution; exile; various corporal punishments, ranging in severity from whipping and branding to public display in stocks; fines; or forced labor. But I don't want to leave the impression that corporal punishment predominated. A study of sentencing in Massachusetts colonies over a sixty-year period (1630–1692) tallied only fifty-six death sentences and nearly three times as many fines as corporal punishments.[6]

Execution was by hanging, but while many crimes were deemed capital, relatively few miscreants were actually executed. Pardons, mock executions, and the so-called benefit of clergy saved many from the gallows.[7] The colonies also repudiated English law providing the death penalty for property crimes, making colonial law much more lenient.[8] Those put to death were hanged in public and solemn occasions attended by everyone in the area, accompanied by sermons, hymn singing, and expressions of penitence by the condemned if he hoped for heavenly salvation. The actual hanging could be slow and excruciatingly painful, depending on such things as the length of the rope and the height of the gallows. If your neck was broken and spine severed by the drop, you were lucky, as death was instantaneous; if you died of asphyxiation, it would be a long and torturous end.[9]

The most brutal execution methods were used on slaves who rebelled or conspired to. As a result of the New York slave conspiracies of 1712 and 1741, sixteen blacks were burned alive, one was hanged in chains, and another was broken on the wheel.[10] In Virginia, between 1706 and 1784, 555 slaves were sentenced to hang, mostly (56 percent) for stealing or arson. Their owners were compensated for the loss by the colonial authorities.[11]

Banishment as a penal sanction meant being sent off to another colony, not abroad. In the Massachusetts Bay Colony, it was a discretionary alternative to death for a second heresy offense or the third conviction for burglary and robbery.[12] Banishment *to* America proved far more significant than expulsion *from* the colonies. In the eighteenth century criminal exiles from abroad, along with an increase in slaves and indentured servants, enlarged the colonial population. An estimated fifty thousand felons were "transported," as the punishment was called, from the United Kingdom to the colonies between 1718 and 1775. This probably caused a rise in crime here, followed by the imposition of more severe punishments, especially near the end of the colonial era.[13]

Corporal punishments were common in the colonies, especially for the poor, who could not afford fines or restitution. Whipping was the most frequent, carried out at a whipping post visible to anyone in the center of town. Thirty-nine lashes, per biblical injunction,[14] were imposed for serious crimes, such as rape or counterfeiting, with the number reduced for less odious offenses. Occasionally, the guilty were "whipt at the carts taile," that is, stripped to the waist and tied to the back of a cart, where they were lashed as they passed through the town to the jeers of spectators. Other bodily punishments included branding (*A* for adulterer, *B* for burglar, etc.), nailing of ears to the pillory or the cutting off of ears altogether, and the placing of a cleft stick on the tongue for swearing or a heavy lock on the leg of a runaway servant.[15]

Shaming was intended to humiliate the offender, but also to reintegrate him into the community. So, for instance, a truly penitent lawbreaker might be required to acknowledge his wrongdoing before the congregation and then be returned to the fold. The unrepentant might have a letter of infamy branded on his body or be forced to wear a letter on her clothes (like Hester Prynne in Nathaniel Hawthorne's *Scarlet Letter*).

It's entirely possible that these shaming punishments worked—for a time. Once American cities grew, starting in the second half of the eighteenth century, their anonymity defeated such strategies. As public sanctions became less effective, punishing behind closed doors—in prisons—replaced them.

At the lower end of the pain scale were fines and forced labor, along with various bonds and recognizances. Fines were widely utilized by the colonials, especially for more affluent lawbreakers. If a poor offender couldn't pay, he would have to suffer corporal punishments instead. Some colonies expressly exempted "gentlemen" from whipping, so fines were their principal penalty. If the accused was an indentured servant, compelled to work off a debt for a set number of years, extending the term of service might be the sanction.[16] The bias against the poor was blatant.

Bonds and recognizances were frequently posted by an affluent supporter (or family member) who served as a guarantor of good behavior for a stated period, such as a year. The incentive was financial; if the offender deviated again, the bond would be forfeit.[17]

While non-corporal punishments were common in colonial America, public humiliation and painful bodily ordeals remained characteristic. The suffering they wrought was great and certainly unacceptable in our day. We would also view the intermixing of religion and the criminal code as anachronistic and probably a violation of the constitutional separation of church and state as well.

The next chapter describes the birth of the prison, greeted as a great advance over the "sanguinary" codes of the pre-constitutional era. As you'll see, the reforms proved every bit as cruel in their own way.

2

THE SILENT TREATMENT:
BIRTH OF THE PENITENTIARY

WHEN THE POPULATION OF THE AMERICAN COLONIES increased elevenfold in the eighteenth century, crime rose too, and the old maim-and-shame sanctions became ineffectual.[1] Embarrassment and humiliation in front of neighbors was no disincentive to crime where the residents were unknown to one another. Plus, the public, especially middle- and upper-class individuals, was growing increasingly disturbed by corporal punishments and the physical agonies they caused. The revulsion against bodily punishments even triggered an anti-death penalty movement after the American Revolution. Capital punishment, the abolitionists argued, was for European monarchies, not a republic like the post-1776 United States.

The problem was what to replace corporal punishment with. In the

1780s and 1790s, reformist notions of penology caught fire, the latest buzz favoring punishment in private, through the use of solitude and isolation from society.

The main proponent was Benjamin Rush, a physician, enthusiastic supporter of the revolution—he signed the Declaration of Independence—and one of the major social activists of the period. Rush and fellow reformers—many of them Quakers, who advanced a more "modern," egalitarian, Christianity—advocated a new way of dealing with criminals.[2]

They were to be placed in a long-term facility and kept in solitude— what we nowadays would call solitary confinement. This was supposed to reorder their mental capacities and lead to reformation or rehabilitation. Criminals, the activists thought, weren't products of a personal failure to manage original sin or resist satanic temptations. That was the old view. Rush and his fellow reformers believed that social pressures had disordered the mind of the offender, or, as one contemporary historian put it, "deranged one's inner gyroscope."[3] It followed that isolation from society, in a new environment, would reform the criminal.

This view wasn't well thought-out. Just which social pressures caused criminality, and how did they affect the individual? And since not all people were vulnerable to these forces, why were some particularly susceptible? Even more important, how would a change of environment work, and how long would the criminal have to be isolated from these injurious social pressures before he could resist them once released? The failure to answer these questions, or even ask them, led to disastrous consequences for the new penology.

Before we scoff at our benighted ancestors, we might consider a few parallels to our own time. First, the reformers did advance the analysis of human behavior. Current secular thought also rejects the role of original sin and temptation in explaining crime, or to take it out of a religious context, the notion that crime is purely a matter of individual irresponsibility. And contemporary social science accepts the argument that social forces (poverty, weak family structure, or ineffectual community controls, etc.) go far in explaining crime. Late-eighteenth-century reformers, like their contemporary counterparts, also wanted to make criminal justice institutions less punitive (though some current-day activists want to go further and remove criminals from prison altogether). We might ask, however, how exactly these reforms would reduce crime or rehabilitate and reintegrate criminals—the very question that Benjamin Rush and his fellow activists never really confronted.

In the last decade of the eighteenth century, Rush's home state of Pennsylvania took the lead in restructuring penology. Legislators, prominent professionals and businessmen, and liberal Christians spearheaded the effort to replace the death penalty with a penitentiary.[4] In 1790, the legislature endorsed "unremitted solitude" accompanied by hard labor as the treatment most likely to succeed. Four years later Pennsylvania eliminated capital punishment for all crimes except murder in the first degree. Even murder, if considered less wicked, could be reduced to a noncapital offense in reformist Pennsylvania.

Philadelphia then remodeled its Walnut Street Jail by adding sixteen single six-by-eight-foot cells, each with a mattress and a small window above the inmate's reach. There was no bed, table, or bench. The walls were so thick that speech from or to the outside could not be understood. The prisoner was allowed one meal per day and was eventually permitted to read the Bible. All inmates were expected to work, whether housed in the isolation cells or the general population areas. At first, the solitary cells were used for disciplining unruly inmates, but eventually they were reserved for the most serious offenders, including those from other counties in Pennsylvania. Those convicted of major crimes, previously capital offenses, might be required to spend half their sentences in solitary. Thus began America's first prison.[5]

By 1805, New York, New Jersey, Connecticut, Virginia, and Massachusetts had established penitentiaries using solitary confinement in some manner. Even England and France were smitten by the concept. Decades later, in 1831, Alexis de Tocqueville and Gustave de Beaumont made a famous tour of American prisons in order to report back to France on American penological ideas and policies worthy of adoption.[6] At that point the initial problems of the penitentiary were well-known and a fresh set of reforms had to be launched.

Walnut Street should have set off alarms. The facility quickly became overcrowded, and silence couldn't be enforced. There was a shortage of work for the inmates, who were kept in their cells with nothing to do. Legislators grew concerned about the expense of housing people for years. In the first decades of the nineteenth century, nearly all penitentiaries would face similar problems.

Some take issue with the designation of Walnut Street as America's first prison. They point to the Newgate Prison in Connecticut, formed out of an abandoned copper mine and used to hold Tories, court-martialed American soldiers, and prisoners of war during the revolution. Newgate—named for the notorious prison in London—was more a dungeon than a prison, with occupants kept at the bottom of a mine shaft. After the war and a series of prisoner escapes, Newgate was fortified into one of the harshest prisons anywhere. Inmates were forced to work below ground twelve hours a day from four in the morning until four in the afternoon. Whether at work or asleep, they were chained to their places, handcuffed, and collared.

> Eyewitnesses spoke of the vermin, filth, stench, hard fare, and punishments, and a climate where the prisoners' clothes grew moldy and rotten and fell away from their bodies while their limbs grew stiff with rheumatism. They saw prisoners so heavily ironed by handcuffs and fetters that they could move about only by a short jump or hop and others chained in pairs to wheelbarrows. Men at the smithy were observed wearing iron collars held on chains from the roof. A British traveler, Thomas Anburey, wrote in September 1781, "At a place called Symsbury[, Connecticut] are some copper mines where formerly such offenders . . . as the General Assembly did not choose to punish with death were sent, showing the humanity and mildness of the law: but not in my opinion. They would have shown it more

considerably by hanging up the unfortunate wretch: when in the course of a few months after lingering out a miserable existence, the dissolution of nature puts a period to their pain."[7]

After a fire in 1782, Newgate was abandoned until reopened in 1790, the year of Walnut Street's debut. Twenty-four years later the prison was expanded so inmates could be kept above ground except for additional punishment. But an 1827 report said that conditions were so deplorable that most of the 127 prisoners asked to be sent underground, where at least they had more control over their own activities.[8]

Finally, after fifty-four years, Newgate was discarded by Connecticut, largely because of the expense of maintaining it, though also because liberals criticized its cruelties. In 1827, all of the Newgate inmates were chained together and marched twenty miles to the new Wethersfield Prison, modeled after New York's famous Auburn facility.

Auburn Prison became famous for its novel approach to incarceration: congregate labor in silence by day, isolation in single-person cells by night. But as we'll see, this policy soon developed problems, and Auburn imposed its own cruelties.

In fact, Auburn wasn't New York's first prison. Another Newgate, this one beside the Hudson River in Greenwich Village, preceded it. It was planned and established in 1797 by Thomas Eddy, a Quaker merchant committed to reforming criminals. New York's Newgate was for felons only, housed in fifty-four rooms, each twelve by eighteen feet in size and designed for eight occupants. Eddy believed in hard labor in the prison shops, as well as religious worship and even night classes. He forbade the keepers from striking inmates, instead disciplining by solitary confinement and dietary restrictions.[9]

This Newgate almost worked, a tribute to Eddy's skill and foresight. Still, he resigned in 1804, apparently because of disputes with new inspectors. Eddy's resignation, while unfortunate, wasn't the coup de grâce for Newgate. There were management problems; poor prisoner workmanship (or outright sabotage) on goods sold for profit; inmate interactions that made prisoners worse once released; an indiscriminate mix of offenders, including females and juveniles; and—the biggest problem of all—overcrowding. A crime wave attributable to returning soldiers seeking employment after the War of 1812 added to the admissions, and the overcrowded conditions produced a massive riot in 1818. Flogging was reintroduced the following year.[10]

The New York State legislature determined that it was cheaper to build a new prison than to rehab Newgate, so in 1816 they approved what was to become the most famous prison in the United States—Auburn. Nine years later they funded a second prison near the village of Sing Sing, an institution that gained a well-justified reputation for cruelty.

Before turning to the Auburn experiment, I want to emphasize the irony of allowing harsh discipline in prison. An inmate could now be punished more inhumanely than under the old colonial system. In the past he would have been whipped, then set free. Now, as a historian of the New York prisons pointed out, he "could be sentenced to a long prison term and flogged repeatedly if he did not conform to certain rules under confinement."[11]

The Auburn system was built around strict regimentation, silence, whippings for infractions, and hard labor. "Within an atmosphere of repression, humiliation, and gloomy silence, the Auburn convict performed an incessantly monotonous round of activity." Inmates had to rise with the sun; dress in degrading, striped uniforms; march lockstep (right hand on the shoulder of the man in front of them) to a privy; then march to the workshop until 7:00 or 8:00 a.m., when they would troop to the dining hall for breakfast. No words, no signals, no communication whatsoever was permitted, on pain of a flogging by the ever-watchful guards. Following lunch at noon, the inmates returned to the shops for "silent and unremitting labor" until sundown. They were then given food to take back to their cells, which had to be eaten in solitude. If light was sufficient, the prisoner could read the Bible; other books, newspapers, or even letters from the outside world weren't allowed. Perhaps he could converse with the chaplain if he came by.

Lying down was prohibited until the signal to undress and go to bed. Any sexual release other than masturbation, which was considered mentally unhealthy, also was denied.[12]

The idea was to break the spirit of the inmate, to make him submit utterly to the discipline of the institution. Some thought that education and religious guidance should follow, with the aim of rehabilitation. Others felt that reform was hopeless, and that extracting the prisoner's labor while deterring others was the most that could be expected from hardened criminals.[13]

The forced silence had a narrower aim: to keep the prisoners from corrupting their fellow inmates, making them, in effect, better criminals. Early in Auburn's history discipline began to break down and a legislative commission recommended ratcheting up the isolation system. In 1821, the New York legislature embarked on an experiment. It called for the classification of inmates and authorized the most depraved to be condemned to total silence without work for their full terms. Eighty inmates were locked in their cells day and night without any human contact. Several went mad. One leaped from the fourth tier of the prison when his cell door was opened. Another beat his head against the walls of his cell, causing eye damage. A third cut his veins with a piece of tin. In 1823, the state governor toured Auburn and, disturbed by what he found, issued pardons for most of the eighty men. By the end of 1825, the experiment was terminated. That's when Auburn instituted its modified solitary policy, the one that served as a template for prisons throughout the United States and Europe.[14]

This policy—congregate (group) labor in silence during the day, individual cells in silence at night—continued right into the twentieth century, though with ups and downs in terms of leniency or harshness. Treatment of the prisoner in New York depended on the penal philosophy of the administrators of the various prisons, on state politics, and on public attitudes. In the 1840s, a period of general optimism in the United States, support for liberal prison policies flourished. Reform-minded prison administrators were appointed. Writers and activists blamed society or the community for crime and advocated rehabilitation policies. "Society is answerable for crime," wrote one liberal in the *New York Tribune*, "because it is so negligent of duty." Another argued that "the community is itself, by its neglects and bad usages, in part responsible for the sins of its children, and . . . it owes to the criminal, therefore, aid to reform." There even developed at this time a bogus psychology known as "phrenology," which postulated that various regions of the brain were responsible for crime. Since, according to phrenologists, physical causes, not moral failings, explained lawbreaking, it was wrong to hold the individual fully accountable.[15]

In 1847, near the end of the reform era, the New York legislature prohibited flogging except in self-defense or in response to a prisoner revolt. But when more punitive prison administrators took over, they employed torturous workarounds to the no-whipping edict. One was to yoke the inmate by his neck and wrists to an iron bar across his shoulders. Another was a pronged iron collar fastened around the neck. The most popular punishment was the shower bath, a nineteenth-century version of waterboarding. The prisoner was drenched with two gallons of cold well water, sometimes laden with ice for good measure. Commonly the water was released from a tank above the seated inmate and dumped on his head. In some cases a bowl-like apparatus around his neck would catch the water and drain it slowly so that the victim had to struggle to stay above water. In 1860 alone Sing Sing guards imposed shower baths 161 times.[16]

By the middle of the nineteenth century, the optimism surrounding the penitentiary had faded as New York's prisons ran into a succession of acute problems. There was financial trouble due to unscrupulous contractors for goods made with prison labor. The facilities were growing overcrowded, and attacks on guards, along with outright prisoner riots, were becoming commonplace. Turnover in prison personnel was increasing. Finally, the public lost interest in penal reform, and punitive administrators replaced the reform-minded ones. While the prisons continued to function, and would do so right into the twentieth century, it was clear that the heyday of the penitentiary was over.[17]

* * *

Despite the high hopes that the penitentiary would provide significant penological reform, the cruelties of the colonial maim-and-shame system were, it is clear, simply replaced by a new set of brutalities. There is a world of difference between the treatment of prisoners in the first half of the nineteenth century and the management of prisoners today. The idea of a prison without corporal punishment, which is virtually never used today, would have been unimaginable back then. The use of forced silence as a method of rehabilitation is now considered bizarre and inexplicable, though short stints of solitary confinement for punitive purposes are common. Confinement and isolation of violent gang members in medium-to-long-term prisons—the supermax—is the closest contemporary parallel to the penitentiary. But the notion that prisoners should be permitted such amenities as family and conjugal visitations, libraries, gyms, television, email and internet access, as well as advanced medical care, would have astonished and probably horrified nineteenth-century prison administrators.

Furthermore, the length of time a prisoner spent behind bars, and therefore subjected to cruelty, was also much greater in the early nineteenth century. Today the mean time served is two years and eight months, roughly 54 percent of the typical sentence at Auburn in 1846, which locked up its occupants for an average four years and eleven months.[18] Plus, the only way to get a sentence reduced back then was through a governor's clemency, which was politicized and considered arbitrary and destructive of reform efforts. By comparison, prisoners today have the benefit of "good time" (legislative) sentence reduction, which is a virtually automatic one-third discount for all prisoners, as well as parole, which is granted so frequently that four out of five prisoners serve less than their full terms.

After the Civil War there were renewed efforts to improve the prison system and rehabilitate the inmates, especially through the so-called reformatory movement. Many of these reforms—inmate education; physical improvements in cells; good time laws; separate facilities for women, juveniles, and misdemeanants; and indeterminate sentences (allowing for early release of rehabilitated prisoners)—were adopted in some of the states in the second half of the nineteenth century and became generally accepted in the twentieth.[19] But these reforms were limited to a handful of states north of the Mason-Dixon line. In the South, by contrast, a whole new set of penal brutalities, part of the suppression of African Americans, flourished.

3

BLACK GULAG: CONVICT LEASE

CRUEL AS THE PENITENTIARY WAS, it can't compare to the utter viciousness of the convict lease system, used mainly on African Americans in the post-Civil War South. Douglas Blackmon, who called his searing account of the practice *Slavery by Another Name*, hardly exaggerated.[1] Of course, slavery was for life, whereas the lease was for a term of years. On the other hand, slaves were cared for enough to provide labor to their masters while black convicts often died under the most horrific conditions because they could readily be replaced at no cost.

For half a century, from the late 1860s through the first decades of the twentieth century, convict work camps were scattered throughout the South, like some vast black gulag. Businessmen from North and South contracted with state governments for convict labor, which they managed in exchange for monies paid into state coffers and toward fees for county officers. It was a real bargain. In Alabama, for example, from 1891 to 1903, nearly seven hundred men were leased to a mining company for around six dollars a month per convict. In Georgia, 1874, one hundred prisoners were leased to another mining business for five years at a measly eleven dollars per convict per year. Most of these men—and many were mere teenagers—were forced to work below ground in dangerous mine shafts, where illness, accidents, brutal punishments (for not producing enough), and killings by fellow inmates decimated the population.[2]

Leasing was a bargain for the state too. States that didn't lease earned around one-third of the cost of running prisons from in-house convict labor. Lease systems took in 267 percent of expenses. In other words, lease states actually made money from their penal systems. In 1886, profitable mining states Alabama and Tennessee each grossed $100,000 from leases, around 10 percent of their state budgets.[3]

County governments also benefited financially. The county courts collected fees for arresting and trying criminal defendants, though the misdemeanor trials were perfunctory, with formalities barely observed. County sheriffs and deputies, who were unsalaried, collected fees plus expenses for each man brought to the local contracting company. These were added to the fines imposed on the convicted defendant, which he, invariably unable to pay, had to work off, thus extending his sentence. For sheriffs and deputies, compensated as the prisoner worked down his fines, this was a major source of income. On top of this were illegal kickbacks to state prison officials for providing various benefits to contractors as well as rewards for whites for turning in alleged transgressors of color.[4] The financial incentives to perpetuate the system are obvious.

The lease began as a stopgap in the face of the destruction of the Southern prison system during the Civil War. Before the war Southern penitentiaries had been nearly all white. In the 1850s whites were over 90 percent of the inmates in Tennessee, Alabama, Georgia, Kentucky, and Mississippi. Georgia had not one person of color in its prison. Virginia and Maryland alone housed free persons of color, and

Louisiana seems to have been the only state that imprisoned slaves.[5] Since slaves were property, not citizens, the ordinary criminal laws and penal processes did not apply to them. Their transgressions usually were punished on the plantation, mainly by flogging, though truly serious offenses, such as assaulting a white or burning property, were tried in special courts. If the adjudicated slave was convicted and executed or transported (exiled), the state compensated the owner.[6] But slaves who died due to accident, disease, or homicide were simply an economic loss to the slaveholder. When, after the war, convicts were leased, death or inability to work due to injury or illness didn't matter to the lessee; he simply got a replacement.

The war destroyed Southern penitentiaries. Mississippi sent its prisoners to Alabama. Arkansas dispersed its inmates throughout the state. Georgia freed them if they agreed to fight for the Confederacy. They deserted, and General Sherman burned the prison. When the Confederate army abandoned Richmond, prisoners ransacked the Virginia penitentiary and set it ablaze.[7]

Though the Southern states had planned to rebuild their prisons, the war created such economic devastation that state revenues collapsed while postwar crime spiked. As a temporary expedient, some states offered convicts to planters and railroads for employment outside prison walls. No one, Republican or Democrat, reconstructionist or redemptionist, black or white, opposed the lease in these early years.[8]

By the 1870s the convict lease system had become profitable and institutionalized. Now that the slaves were free, the state was responsible for black lawbreakers. Except that the laws were broad and vague enough to enable local judges and juries to impose special restrictions on blacks while ignoring many of the white transgressions. Hazy vagrancy statutes (applicable to anyone without steady employment) and strict labor contract laws (tying blacks to the plantations at which they worked) facilitated arrests of African Americans for minor offenses, arrests driven more by economic and race suppression motives than by criminal justice priorities.

Before long the nearly all-white prisoner population was replaced by a nearly all-black one. The number of convicts surged throughout the post-Civil War South. Convict lease produced a tenfold increase in the prison population of Georgia in four decades. North Carolina's state convict population was 121 in 1870, 1,302 in 1890. Florida, Mississippi, and Alabama showed comparable gains in the number of prisoners.[9]

The lease increased the number of convicts but reduced their ages. A sample of Georgia convicts sheds light on the age decline. From 1816 to 1853 about one-quarter of the prisoners were between ages twenty-two and twenty-five, and only 17 percent were ages sixteen to twenty-one. In 1896, when leasing was in full swing, 38 percent of the convicts were sixteen to twenty-one, and the percentage of twenty-two to twenty-five-year-olds actually declined to 22 percent. Half of the 1896 Georgia convicts were minors; some were mere boys, between twelve and fifteen.[10] Throughout the South, anywhere from two-thirds to over three-quarters of leased prisoners were in their twenties or younger.[11]

Despite variations, the states all followed a similar formula for conducting the lease. Each state would negotiate an agreement with some business, such as a plantation, a mining company, or a railroad, in need of laborers. The amount paid would cover a certain number of inmates per month or year for an agreed-upon number of years. Each county, in charge of defendants from arrest to conviction, provided the inmates in exchange for fees for the sheriffs and deputies. Once he was turned over to the businesses, about seventy-two hours after arrest, the company took complete charge of the inmate, providing food and clothing and preventing escapes. "On paper," as Douglas Blackmon explained, "the regulations governing convict conditions required that prisoners receive adequate food, be provided with clean living quarters, and be protected from 'cruel' or 'excessive punishment.'" But the reality was far different.

> Company guards were empowered to chain prisoners, shoot those attempting to flee, torture any who wouldn't submit, and whip the disobedient—naked or clothed—almost without limit. Over eight

decades, almost never were there penalties to any acquirer of these slaves for their mistreatment or deaths.[12]

The mistreatment was enough to turn your stomach. An 1882 article in the *New York Times* described conditions at an Alabama coal mine, telling of

> black prisoners packed into a single cramped cabin like slaves on the Atlantic passage. The building had no windows. Vermin-ridden bunks stacked three high were covered with straw and "ravaged blankets." "Revoltingly filthy" food was served cold from unwashed coal buckets, and all 150 black convicts shared three half-barrel tubs for washing. All convicts were forced to wear shackles consisting of an "iron hoop fastened around the ankle to which is attached a chain two feet long and terminating in a ring."[13]

In an incident described at a legislative hearing in Alabama in 1881, a witness, Jonathan D. Goode, described a prisoner who had escaped but, with the aid of bloodhounds, was recaptured. The mine owner forced him to lie on the ground with the dogs biting him.

> "He begged piteously to have the dogs taken off of him, but Comer [the mine owner] refused to allow it."
> Then Comer "took a stirrup strap, doubled it and wet it, stripped him naked, bucked him, and whipped him—unmercifully whipped him, over half an hour. The Negro begged them to take a gun and kill him," Goode continued. "They left him in a Negro cabin where . . . he died within a few hours."[14]

Some inmate overseers preferred the water treatment to severe whipping since the prisoner could return to work quicker after the punishment. The restrained inmate, undoubtedly terrified, had a continuous stream of water poured on his lips and nose until he thought he would drown.[15]

Disturbing late-nineteenth-century investigations and news reports graphically depicted the horrors of the lease system, yet the gross injustices hardly changed in the South for several more decades. Consider Blackmon's account of the arrest in 1908 of Green Cottenham, a twenty-two-year-old African American.

Cottenham was charged in Shelby County, Alabama, with vagrancy (essentially, lack of employment), and after three days in jail was found guilty by a county judge and sentenced to thirty days of hard labor. After fees were tacked on—for the sheriff, his deputy, the court clerk, and witnesses—Cottenham, unable to pay, had his sentence extended to nearly a year, a typical sentence for a leased misdemeanant. He then was turned over to the Tennessee Coal, Iron & Railroad Company, a subsidiary of United States Steel Corporation, which paid the county $12 a month for Cottenham's fines and fees.[16]

Blackmon describes the rest in chilling detail.

> The company plunged Cottenham into the darkness of a mine called Slope No. 12—one shaft in a vast subterranean labyrinth on the edge of Birmingham known as the Pratt Mines. There, he was chained inside a long wooden barrack at night and required to spend nearly every waking hour digging and loading coal. His required daily "task" was to remove eight tons of coal from the mine. Cottenham was subject to the whip for failure to dig the requisite amount, at risk of physical torture for disobedience, and vulnerable to the sexual predations of other miners—many of whom already had passed years or decades in their own chthonian confinement. The lightless catacombs of black rock, packed with hundreds of desperate men slick with sweat and coated in pulverized coal, must have exceeded any vision of hell a boy born in the countryside of Alabama—even a child of slaves—could have ever imagined.
>
> Waves of disease ripped through the population. In the month before Cottenham arrived at the prison mine, pneumonia and

tuberculosis sickened dozens. Within his first four weeks, six died. Before the year was over, almost sixty men forced into Slope 12 were dead of disease, accidents, or homicide. Most of the broken bodies, along with hundreds of others before and after, were dumped into shallow graves scattered among the refuse of the mine. Others were incinerated in nearby ovens used to blast millions of tons of coal brought to the surface into coke—the carbon-rich fuel essential to U.S. Steel's production of iron.

Noting the irony of emancipation less than half a century earlier, Blackmon concluded:

> Forty-five years after President Abraham Lincoln's Emancipation Proclamation freeing American slaves, Green Cottenham and more than a thousand other black men toiled under the lash at Slope 12. Imprisoned in what was then the most advanced city of the South, guarded by whipping bosses employed by the most iconic example of the modern corporation emerging in the gilded North, they were slaves in all but name.[17]

As one might imagine, the mortality figures for leased convicts were shocking, though much depended on the type of work assignment imposed. The United States as a whole had a prison mortality rate of 25 per 1,000. In Texas, it was 49 per 1,000 for those leased to plantations, 54 for those sent to iron works, 74 for prisoners put to work on railroads, and 250 for every thousand forced to labor in the swamps of eastern Texas. In 1870 in Alabama, where dangerous mining was prevalent, 41 percent of 180 convicts died. Of course, mortality figures don't tell us about the uncounted broken bodies from illness, assault, and accident, no doubt more numerous than even the deaths.[18]

By the last decades of the nineteenth century, convict leasing was starting to run into economic problems. These problems intensified in the twentieth century, resulting in the demise of the lease. First, free laborers complained bitterly that prisoners were taking their jobs and suppressing wages to boot. Tennessee, a major mining state, was the first to face difficulties when free miners protested, went on strike numerous times, and revolted by loading the convicts and their guards on trains to keep them out of the mines. By 1895, the governor decided that the expense of protecting convict labor wasn't worth the benefit, and Tennessee abolished convict leasing.

By the 1890s five southern states had created penal farms to remove especially vulnerable and unproductive workers from the lease, namely, women, children, and the infirm. But only three states—Louisiana, Mississippi, and Tennessee—abolished leasing altogether. At the end of the century, nine states were still forcing convicts into labor camps.[19]

In 1903, the United States attorney for Alabama launched a federal investigation into the use of force by private individuals to compel labor, a violation of the anti-peonage laws. Despite several successful prosecutions and support from President Theodore Roosevelt's administration, Alabama's all-white juries were, to put it mildly, unsympathetic to the government's case, and leasing continued right up to 1927.[20]

The economic problems with the lease grew more acute as the twentieth century progressed. First, the price of convicts kept increasing, while the depressions of 1893 and 1907 eliminated shortages of labor. Second, the long-term decline in the agricultural sector, worsened by a rabid boll weevil infestation, reduced the need for farm workers. And third, mechanized coal mining, developed by the 1920s, made manual labor mines obsolete.

These developments, combined with the scandals, well publicized in the media, especially in the North, meant the end of convict leasing in all states except Alabama by 1920. There was one other factor in the abolition: the southern states realized that prisoners could be required to work on roads and other public projects. Leasing convicts to private businesses was replaced by chain gangs working for the state or county.[21] We pick up that story in chapter 5.

4

PROGRESSIVES

VIRTUALLY EVERY CONTEMPORARY penological leniency you can think of can be traced back to the Progressive Era, which ran from the 1890s to around 1920. The list includes probation, parole, indeterminate sentencing, in-prison educational and vocational programs, and a separate juvenile justice system. Though the reforms didn't quite work as planned, they had staying power and are still very much in use in our current system.

Progressivism in criminal justice traces its launch to an 1870 Cincinnati conference dubbed the National Congress on Penitentiary and Reformatory Discipline.[1] The conference—one of the seminal events in American penological history—gathered all the key players in the reform movement, including Reverend Enoch Wines and Zebulon Brockway, who soon would get to put into practice the principles drawn up by the participants.

The guiding principle of the conference was rehabilitation: "the supreme aim of prison discipline is the reformation of criminals, not the infliction of vindictive suffering."[2] Reform was to be achieved by such policies as:

- indeterminate sentencing, meaning no fixed maximum sentence, enabling a prisoner to be released as soon as he is rehabilitated;

- a system of "marks" or grades measuring a prisoner's progress toward eligibility for release;

- religious services, academic classes, and vocational training; and

- "steady, active, honorable labor" within the prison.

The conferees also called for prisons to provide sanitary conditions, including sufficient light, space, and ventilation, and denounced degrading punishments.[3] The call for more wholesome conditions was, of course, incompatible with the old fortress-style penitentiaries, which, given the expense of replacement, would remain in use well into the twentieth century.

Indeterminate sentencing and its adjunct, parole (not spelled out in the Cincinnati principles), started catching on in the late 1800s. Indeterminate sentencing, which replaced determinate or fixed sentences (*x* years, no more or less, for a crime), was ideal for believers in rehabilitation. It worked as follows: A minimum to be served, typically one year, was mandated by the statutes, but not a maximum. The ultimate release date would be determined by the prison authorities instead of the judge. The idea was that the prison management (later, a parole board, usually appointed by state governors) would closely monitor the inmate's behavior and determine when he was sufficiently reformed to be trusted with freedom. New York passed such a law in 1877, and other states followed.[4] By 1927 nearly half of all released prisoners (49 percent) were paroled, while 42 percent had completed full (determinate) sentences.[5]

Another nineteenth-century innovation was to shorten sentences through "good time" laws. With good time the legislature determined how much a sentence could be reduced. It was intended that the prison administrators could grant it or not depending on the inmate's behavior. However, it quickly degenerated into an entitlement as administrators tallied the convict's good time discount (based on the length of his sentence) and applied it when he first entered the prison. Front-ending the discount eliminated most of the inmate's incentive, especially since taking the benefit away was more complicated for the administrators than leaving it in place. By 1876 twenty-nine states and the federal government had adopted some sort of good time law, but despite its staying power, good time was eclipsed in usefulness as a penological tool by parole.[6]

In the first decades of the twentieth century, penologists, imbued with the Progressive spirit, were optimistic about parole. The legendary Wickersham Commission, which was highly critical of the criminal justice system of the early 1930s, called parole "a method of [crime] prevention second to none."[7] But the Commission acknowledged that it was hard to be sure that someone is truly rehabilitated—the main defect in the policy. As the commissioners conceded, "it is the universal testimony of penal administrators that the most dangerous of criminals to society invariably maintain the best of prison records."[8] In the twenty-first century, even with our long experience with parole and our sophisticated analytical tools, we haven't gotten much better at predicting who will or won't recidivate. A recent study found that five out of six released state prisoners were arrested again.[9]

Of course, it's cheaper to release prisoners, especially in a time of rising crime, such as the 1920s, than to build new prisons. On the other hand, parole officers cost money too, and the crime prevention benefits of the parole system depend on having enough trained agents to properly monitor the released prisoners. This seldom happened. Appointments of officers were made through political patronage, and training usually was inadequate. In 1930 New York there were only 12 full-time parole officers for about 2,000 parolees, 167 per officer, though they did get help from volunteers affiliated with charitable organizations. The Kansas parole agency was even more understaffed: in 1937 it had 8 officers for 2,151 parolees, a whopping 269 per officer.[10]

Still, parole became a mainstay of the justice system because it prevents prison overcrowding without the expense of building new facilities, and inmates have come to rely on it. It also provided an alternative to gubernatorial clemency, which was arbitrary and often corrupt.

During the crime wave of the 1920s and early 1930s, the public blamed parole for contributing to the problem by coddling offenders. But analysts denied this because, they reasoned, the state is actually adding to the controls over convicts by intruding into their lives after release. "Parole is not leniency," said the Wickersham Commission. "On the contrary, parole really increases the State's period of control."[11] Though control in prison is far more certain and intrusive than control in the community, it is conceivable that prisoners were kept in longer under a parole system since the parole authorities answered to no one when determining who was to be released. By contrast, under a determinate sentencing scheme, the sentencing judge was prohibited from imposing a sentence stiffer than the one set forth in the statutes. With indeterminate sentencing the prisoner would theoretically be released once reformed. But who could say when that point was reached?

A census report on prisoners discharged in 1926 showed that parolees served a bit longer (two years and forty-four days on average) than prisoners given a determinate sentence (one year and nine months), but the difference may not have been due to indeterminate sentencing. The states without the "modern" reform usually were in the South, where sentences were longer regardless of the sentencing scheme.[12]

Not all the laws passed during the Progressive Era afforded leniency, even in northern states. Recidivists faced stiffer sentences pursuant to so-called habitual criminal laws, which upped the ante considerably for repeat offenders. Ohio, for example, passed legislation in 1885 that imposed a natural life sentence on anyone committing a third felony—even if the third offense standing alone would have netted the defendant no more than a few years.[13] This kind of law may sound familiar as a forerunner to California's well-known "Three Strikes" law of 1994.[14]

The jewel in the crown of progressivism was the reformatory, exemplified by the Elmira facility in New York. Zebulon Brockway, who electrified the 1870 Cincinnati conference with his progressive ideas on penology, was appointed superintendent of Elmira, which opened in 1876. Elmira was Brockway's chance to put his ideas into action, and he was convinced that his policies could reform offenders. The New York legislature was supportive, limiting Elmira's population to first offenders ages sixteen to thirty. This helped Brockway because he didn't have to prove himself with hardened criminals and recidivists.[15]

In some ways the routine for Elmira inmates was no different than at Auburn, prison labor serving as the centerpiece. Prisoners were awakened by guards at 5:15 in the morning, given fifteen minutes to dress, and were expected to clean their cells. They then had breakfast and were sent to work in the shops from 7:30 a.m. until 4:30 p.m., with an hour off for lunch at noon. In keeping with the belief in education, lectures by visitors were sometimes offered in the evening, and inmates were required to attend classes at 7:00 p.m. The classes covered basics such as reading, writing, and math, but there also were more advanced courses in history, geography, and composition. On Sundays, consistent with the religiosity of the period, there were mandatory services.

The big difference with the previous system of punishment was indeterminate sentencing and parole, which enabled the prisoner to gain release through good behavior as measured by Brockway's innovative system of "marks." The Elmira evaluation system worked this way: Inmates were grouped into one of three classifications, with new entrants being placed in grade two. If the new prisoners complied with Elmira's rules for six months, they would be promoted to grade one. Grade one prisoners got better treatment, such as comfortable blue uniforms, spring mattresses, better food, and the like. Most important, six months of good marks in grade one meant a parole hearing; in other words, an inmate could be released in a year. A new admit who didn't comply with the rules would be demoted to grade three: coarse red uniforms, lockstep movement, and no mail, library privileges, or visitations. Each inmate was evaluated monthly and given marks for performance in classes, at work, and in general comportment. The mark system was touted as a "scientific-empirical" measure of each inmate's progress toward reform.[16]

Throughout its first decade (the 1880s) Elmira continued to innovate. A gym was built and team sports were introduced. Military drills and calisthenics were included in the regimen. Instruction in trades was enhanced so that by 1896 there were thirty-six different offerings. Even the evaluation system got an upgrade. Instead of marks, inmates were paid wages based on the quality of their work, satisfactory completion of courses, and good comportment, while being charged for room and board, doctor's visits, and fines for misbehavior. The financial support for this came from businesses that contracted with the facility.[17]

Brockway launched a publicity campaign to promote Elmira; as a result, the facility, along with its founder, became internationally known. By the start of the twentieth century, ten reformatories had opened in the United States, with populations too old for juvenile institutions, but less dangerous than maximum security prisons. By 1920, eighteen states and the federal government had reformatories.[18]

Did Elmira work? The most straightforward measure is the success or failure of the men it released, that is, whether or not they committed new crimes. On this score the returns are very positive, maybe suspiciously so. Early studies found that over 80 percent of Elmira's graduates went on to lead law-abiding lives.[19] But a famous fifteen-year study of inmates released from the Massachusetts Reformatory in 1921 or 1922 found that only one-third desisted altogether while 61 percent engaged in more crime.[20] Some contemporary critics discount or denigrate the low recidivism rates attributed to Elmira. They charge that Elmira's real purpose was "repression, not reform," aimed at "transforming America's new dangerous classes into law-abiding and socially and economically productive working-class citizens." But they offer no proof that Brockway or other reformers ever endorsed class repression or transformation.[21]

If Elmira had produced significant numbers of law-abiding and socially productive ex-convicts, it would seem to have been a rehabilitationist's dream. But there is one fly in the ointment. The overwhelming majority of Elmira's inmates had been convicted of relatively minor crimes, offenses that probably would result in a sentence of probation nowadays, especially for first offenders (and the vast majority of Elmira's entrants were first offenders). For example, a report on the crimes of new admissions to Elmira in 1915 indicates that fully one-third had been convicted of the lowest-level burglary and 17 percent were in for second-degree grand larceny.[22] Given such inmates, it is likely that comparable rehabilitation could have been achieved without any incarceration at all. In other words, Elmira may have overpunished by taking in offenders who did not need to be incarcerated.[23]

In addition, not all of Elmira's policies were successful or even acceptable. Two policies were especially egregious. First, Elmira sterilized certain prisoners with mental deficiencies, part of a eugenics policy that many well-meaning reformers championed in the Progressive Era. Second was the use of corporal punishment, even by Brockway himself, a practice that ultimately destroyed his career.

During the Progressive Era it was commonly believed that large proportions of criminals were "mentally defective" and that the defects were inherited. Books such as *The Kallikak Family* by prominent psychologist and eugenicist H. H. Goddard tracked generations of offenders within the same family. Goddard found that Martin Kallikak, a Revolutionary War soldier, produced law-abiding descendants with his Quaker wife, but also fathered the first of many generations of criminals in an illicit affair with a "nameless feeble-minded woman" whom he'd met in a tavern. In a subsequent book Goddard contended that "at least 50 percent of all criminals are mentally defective," and endorsed eugenics as a policy solution.[24]

Since crime, progressives believed, was due to multiple causes, including biological traits, measures to prevent reproduction by mental defectives would reduce illegality, spare from punishment a person not fully responsible, and improve the quality of subsequent generations. The eugenics movement, pushed by liberal reformers (not, as you might think, conservatives), considered involuntary sterilization a perfectly rational and socially beneficial solution to the crime problem. The eugenicists would no doubt be aghast to learn that their campaign is now universally condemned as the precursor to Nazi eugenics for racial purification.

Several progressive-oriented reformatories, including Elmira, instituted a sterilization policy. Surgical vasectomies for mentally deficient inmates who were thought to be unreformable were first undertaken at the Indiana reformatory, then at the Elmira and the Massachusetts facilities. The Indiana reformatory physician performed 382 sterilizations, presumably involuntary, between 1899 and 1906. Indiana passed the nation's first compulsory sterilization law in 1907. Within a decade thirteen states had adopted similar laws, which the Supreme Court upheld.[25] But the use in prisons didn't advance without some sharp criticisms among penologists and practitioners. One warden called it "damnable," adding, "It is dangerous. It is inhuman and it is unchristian." Most state reformatories in the United States declined to resort to sterilizations.[26]

It wasn't eugenics that did Brockway in, however; it was corporal punishment. In 1893, New York's State Board of Charities, a watchdog group that had been monitoring prisons, issued a blistering report on Brockway's management of Elmira. They accused him of "unlawful, unjust, cruel, brutal, inhuman, degrading, excessive, and unusual punishment of inmates, frequently causing permanent injuries and disfigurements."[27] Specifically, Brockway was alleged to have struck an inmate with his fist, kicked another when he was on the floor, put salt in paddling wounds if the inmate failed to cry out, put a man on bread and water for nineteen months and put rings on his penis when he requested a transfer, and had men thrown into vats of boiling water. The Board of Charities charged that the paddling of inmates, which Brockway himself administered, had increased to 1,396 in 1892 alone. A later investigation found that Brockway used a leather strap on misbehaving prisoners, placed them in solitary, and shackled them to cell beds or doors.[28] In keeping with attitudes of the time, however, the board, while condemning the excesses alleged, did not disapprove of corporal punishment.

The newspapers quickly picked up the story, and the yellow journalism of the day gave Brockway a steady drubbing. The *New York Times* alone published over one hundred articles on the allegations. Brockway defended the paddlings, contending that they were necessary for order in the facility. He also pointed out that the complaining inmates had been troublemakers transferred to other prisons. The Elmira staff and board of managers stood by their beleaguered superintendent. In 1894, as a result of a second investigation, the assertions of the pro-Brockway managers were borne out and many of the inmates' charges were shown to have been false or exaggerated. The Charities Board was stripped of its watchdog duties over prisons. Despite the superintendent's exoneration, governor Theodore Roosevelt appointed a new board of managers for Elmira in 1899. The board levied fresh charges against Brockway, including allegations of financial misdealing, and started replacing the reformatory's top management. By 1900, Brockway, now seventy-three, had succumbed to the pressure and turned in his resignation.

This was not the end of Elmira, nor of the reform movement. In fact, reformatories thrived over the first two decades of the twentieth century. However, they varied from state to state in their policies and the quality of their administrations. Some emphasized rehabilitation through Elmira-type programs; others stressed punishment and profit.[29] Starting in the 1920s, however, there was a steady rise in crime, partly as a result of Prohibition, and a concomitant growth in prisoners, including more recidivists. This made rehabilitation programs difficult to maintain.[30] Homicide rates hit historic highs, unequaled in the twentieth century until the 1970s.[31] State and federal prison admissions rose an eye-popping 76 percent between 1923 and 1931.[32] Partly because of the brazenness of the warring booze gangs, the public was convinced that crime was out of control. Confidence in the criminal justice system and belief in the rehabilitation of criminals evaporated. (A similar thing happened in the 1970s in the face of the massive crime wave of that era—a matter addressed in part 2.)

Starting in the 1920s, reformatories lost their distinctiveness and became just like any other prison. The reality is, reformatories didn't produce reform any more than penitentiaries produced penitents. But the lenient policies spawned by progressivism—probation, parole, indeterminate sentencing, and (to a lesser extent) educational, vocational, and therapeutic programs for inmates—became enduring parts of the American criminal justice system.

5

SOUTHERN REGRESSIVISM

PROGRESSIVISM NORTHERN-STYLE was met with skepticism in the South. Partly this was due to racist beliefs that African Americans, who furnished a big percentage of criminal defendants, were not good candidates for reform. Race aside, southerners simply were more punitive than Yankees; they believed in retribution and deterrence, but not so much in rehabilitation. Another reason was money. The South was America's impoverished stepchild before World War II, and the funds for Elmira-style reforms, with more highly trained and better-paid staff, simply were unavailable. Still, there were improvements in the southern justice system in the first decades of the twentieth century, and prisoner death rates declined significantly with the demise of the convict lease.

The year-round temperate climate of the South produced a new cost-saving idea for managing convicts. Prison farms and road-work gangs became the centerpiece of the southern justice system. They didn't totally replace prisons, but since they generated income, while penitentiaries were costly, more convicts were channeled to the prison farms or road gangs than to the traditional prison.

By around 1910 most southern states had ended the convict lease. The brutalities of the lease had generated disturbing press exposés, and the changing economy, with more mechanized labor, made leasing unprofitable for business. Of course, brutalities could and did occur even with state- or county-owned operations. But since the private contractors under the lease system had no stake in the health or welfare of convicts, whom they could readily replace, mortality rates declined, probably cruelty as well, with the rise of prison farms and road gangs.

African Americans made up much of the southern prisoner population. This is only partly explained by bias. Blacks, like white southerners, had exceptionally high violent crime rates, and the racial bias played out in leniency for whites more than severity for blacks. In fact, serious black-on-black crime was more likely to be underpunished due to indifference to the victims.[1] However, racism probably accounted for the elevated number of blacks arrested for misdemeanors, and in some states it was minor offenses that fed the South's outdoor justice system. In North Carolina, for example, for every white on the county chain gang in 1926, there were two men of color.[2]

Southern progressives were, at best, partly successful in establishing a more humane environment for convicts or Elmira-like reformation policies. Southerners were more interested in reducing the cost of the system and improving security (preventing escapes) than in "mollycoddling" prisoners.

Texas, for example, alternated between periods of reform and reaction, shifting from convict leasing to state prison farms to greater reliance on prisons. Of course, pendulum swings from conservatism to liberalism and back are commonplace in policymaking; look at penology in our own day. In 1910, following a series of newspaper exposés excoriating the private exploitation of prisoner labor, the state passed a sweeping prison reform bill abolishing leasing. The new law also limited the hours convicts could be made to work in a day, banned Sunday labor, and paid prisoners for work (a paltry ten cents per day). It called for better food, improved medical care, and strict regulation of the women's facility, which had been the subject of scandalous news reports. These reforms added nothing to the state treasury, so Texas, which had purchased land for penal farms in the nineteenth century, still relied on convict labor for revenue. Texas had at this time two penitentiaries and six farms totaling twenty thousand acres. Now more convicts were sent to the state plantations, where, in contrast with the prisons, they could generate income.[3]

It wasn't long before the prisoners grew dissatisfied, especially when the state became cash-strapped and balked at paying them. There were convict mutinies and arsons. Guards and supervisors chafed at the restrictions on their authority. Punishments grew more severe. In one horrifying incident eight black prisoners suffocated to death when twelve men were crammed into a seven-by-nine-foot box. The last straw was flooding, which, in 1913 and 1914, wiped out the penal farm's crops along with the state's profits.[4]

A period of reaction followed. With rising crime in the 1920s and the influential Ku Klux Klan advocating law-and-order policies, reform took a backseat to retribution, deterrence, and of course, production. (The 1920s Klan, unlike its nineteenth-century namesake, was a mainstream rather than a clandestine terrorist operation, but still racist.) Texas centralized control over the death penalty, which had been administered by the counties, and Huntsville became known for its electric chair. This being Texas, Huntsville became even more famous for its prison rodeo, started in 1931.[5]

Galvanized by reports of prisoner whippings and other brutalities, a new reform effort emerged. In 1924, a state Committee on Prisons and Prison Labor issued a lengthy study on the Texas penal system. It declared the state prison farms, now grown to ninety thousand acres, "a complete failure," and called for a central penal colony with several buildings and a farm for inmate food only. Influenced by New York's reform policies, the committee also sought reformatories for women and "more promising" young white offenders (note the racism), a medical and psychiatric clinic, and pay, schooling, and vocational training for inmates.[6]

A Progressive governor, Dan Moody, took office in 1927 and launched a new set of reforms. The ten-hour workday was enforced, some of the brutal guards were fired, religious and educational programs were expanded, and a prisoner organization, the Prison Welfare League, was begun. The League ran rehabilition programs, established prison schools, created an employment center for convicts close to release, and started an inmate newspaper, the *Echo*.[7]

As often happens with reforms, expectations were raised that realities couldn't match. Governor Moody placed a moratorium on clemencies (which had been arbitrary and corrupt) and reduced releases, crowding the facilities and angering the prisoners. A shortage of guards sparked escape attempts and by 1928, 760 prisoners—17 percent of the inmate population, an all-time high—had run off. Moody then appointed Lee Simmons, a hardliner, to manage the system.[8]

"Under Simmons," wrote Robert Perkinson, "New Woman penology was out; manly planter justice was back." Simmons emphasized cash-crop agriculture, ended convict work restrictions, and brought back the whip. He got the legislature to pay for new dormitories and warehouses on a central farm, adding meatpacking and cannery operations to generate income. In short, Texas's second reform effort was over.[9]

The most famous Texas escapees were Bonnie and Clyde, a vicious pair of robber-murderers glamorized by the Hollywood movie bearing their names. Clyde Barrow, first arrested in 1930, when he was twenty-one, was jailed on suspicion of burglary. His girlfriend, Bonnie Parker, a nineteen-year-old waitress, smuggled a gun into the jail, and Clyde escaped along with three other inmates. After a series of robberies, burglaries, and car thefts, Barrow was arrested a second time in 1930, received a fourteen-year sentence, and was sent to the Eastham Prison Farm in Huntsville. He had a fellow inmate cut off two of his toes so he could be transferred to the prison hospital and paroled since he could no longer do farm work. At the time, self-mutilations were becoming common in Texas prisons; there were 174 such acts between 1936 and 1940, and the numbers went up in the 1940s.[10]

Barrow was paroled in 1932 and promptly went on another crime spree, robbing small shops and gas stations and murdering a store manager. In 1933, he planned a prison break for members of his gang held at the Eastham farm. One guard was killed and another wounded, and Bonnie and Clyde drove off with five inmates. Huntsville's director, Lee Simmons, swore that he'd bring his guard's killers to justice. He hired Frank Hamer, a former Texas Ranger, to hunt down the couple. In 1934, following several more robberies, Hamer and a posse ambushed Bonnie and Clyde in Arcadia, Louisiana. Riddling their car with bullets, he killed both of them.[11]

* * *

Perhaps the most notorious of the southern prison farms was Mississippi's Parchman, a forty-six-square-mile plantation in the Yazoo Delta. It was constructed in 1904 by Governor James K. Vardaman, a racist, but also a populist. Vardaman strongly opposed convict leasing, not because of its brutalities, but because, he said, it enriched big planters and railroad barons at public expense. He believed that blacks could learn discipline, good work habits, and respect for white authority in a plantation environment. It was, he believed, a humane and sensible response to black crime.[12]

Early on the great bulk of Mississippi's convicted felons went to Parchman. They were overwhelmingly black, young, and illiterate. A 1917 report stated that African Americans were around 90 percent of the inmate population. Nearly two-thirds of their crimes were serious violent offenses, such as murder, manslaughter, assault, and rape, overwhelmingly victimizing other persons of color. Sentencing in Mississippi was determinate (fixed number of years) with "good time" reductions provided by the legislature. Unlike northern states, Mississippi had no parole release until 1944. By the 1930s Parchman was nearly 30 percent white, due to Prohibition violations in the 1920s and a surge in property crimes during the Depression. Whites were placed in segregated field camps but had the same work regimen as the black inmates.[13]

Parchman certainly didn't look like a prison. There were no massive walls, no guard towers, no cellblocks, or stockades. There was instead a vast expanse of farmland, with cattle barns, vegetable gardens, mules, and miles of cotton. By 1915 it was a self-sufficient operation, with a sawmill, brick manufacture, a slaughterhouse, vegetable canneries, and two cotton gins.

The land was divided into fifteen field camps about one-half mile apart, each surrounded by barbed wire. Every field camp had a "cage": long wooden barracks with barred windows, where inmates ate and slept. Each cage had two dorms, one for trusties, another for all other convicts, separated by a dining area in the middle. The dorms had bunks stacked side by side along the walls.[14]

Parchman was headed by a superintendent, experienced as a farmer, not a prison administrator. He lived in a Victorian mansion near the entrance. The prison staff was made up of rural lower-class whites, little better educated than the men they supervised, most of whom were illiterate.[15] Staff pay was low, but employees had the benefit of a free cottage, free food, and convict servants.

The inmate day began at 4:30 a.m. After a breakfast of biscuits and syrup with coffee, the men were marched to the field. There they worked in a line. A "caller" set the pace for work with a chant that was imitated by the chorus of inmates. (Some of these chants were recorded and are available online.[16]) Each man was expected to pick two hundred pounds of cotton a day, not difficult for an experienced sharecropper. A noon meal consisting of beans, peas, sweet potatoes, salted meat, and a cold drink was eaten in the field, under the sun if there was no shade nearby. The food was often full of bugs, as it was stored in unsanitary conditions. The biggest problem, though, was the brutal Mississippi heat, especially in June. Some inmates collapsed from sunstroke and overwork; some died.[17]

The field drivers (sergeants) carried "Black Annie," a three-foot-long whip, from their belts, employing it to get the men to work. Whipping also was used to punish inmates for infractions such as fighting, stealing, or disrespect to an officer. Some of the guards were alcoholics or sadists, and the floggings, especially for escape attempts, could be extremely brutal. By 1900 corporal punishment of prisoners was abolished by law outside the South (though as we saw, practice was another matter), but most southern states, including Arkansas, Texas, Florida, Louisiana, and Mississippi, permitted lashing.[18]

At the edge of the field stood the trusties, long-term prisoners armed with Winchester rifles. They would shoot anyone who tried to escape, for which they received credit toward parole. The trusties were hardened criminals serving long sentences; often they had personality disorders or mental illness. Their first loyalty was to the staff who appointed them and had the power to recommended release or demotion to ordinary prisoner. They were hated and feared by the other inmates, and if a trusty was demoted, the consequences for him could be lethal. The trusty system was cruel, but since it was cheaper than hiring and training guards, it remained in place until the 1970s, when a federal court finally abolished it.[19]

Trusties were given better food and sleeping quarters, could move about the camp freely, hunt and fish in their spare time, and spend Sundays with wives, girlfriends, or prostitutes from a nearby town. Parchman, believe it or not, was the first U.S. prison to allow conjugal visits. They were held on Sundays in a wooden shack maintained by the convicts in each field camp.[20]

Though trusties, female prisoners, and whites were segregated at Parchman, there wasn't any classification of prisoners by age, seriousness of crime, incorrigibility, or mental condition. "The result," wrote historian David Oshinsky, "was a brutal, predatory culture made worse by the prison's vast and isolated expanse." Young, inexperienced, and minor offenders were thrown in with older, hardened, and vicious convicts. Homosexual assaults on youthful inmates were commonplace, involving by one estimate roughly half the prisoners.[21]

Parchman, in short, was run for profit, not for the improvement of offenders. "Blacks came to Parchman as field workers," Oshinsky lamented, "and left the same way." Where white supremacy and unskilled black labor went hand in hand, he added, "rehabilitation was a dangerous word." Progressive reforms meant little in Mississippi until the 1970s, when they were forced on the state by the federal courts.[22]

* * *

"Bad men make good roads." That was a common refrain in Georgia before the 1920s, and maybe in North Carolina as well. In these states convicts were used to build highways. It was a time when automobiles were coming into popular use and paved roadways were as much an economic necessity as railroad lines had been in the nineteenth century. The road gang, along with the prison farm, were the South's version of Progressive penology. As historian Alex Lichtenstein put it, "the penal road gang was regarded as a quintessential southern Progressive reform, . . . an example of penal humanitarianism, state-sponsored economic mod-ernization and efficiency, and racial moderation."[23]

Georgia and North Carolina had previously relied on a corvée to build roads, under which men from the general population could substitute four or five days of labor annually for certain taxes or fines. This system was a failure, as the amateur labor force had to be closely supervised and the conscripts were less than enthusiastic about working.

Convict leasing to private businesses and road construction gangs employed by the state or counties existed simultaneously around the turn of the century. In 1908 Georgia abolished both the corvée and the lease, relying exclusively on convict road gangs. This produced nearly five thousand felony and misdemeanor convicts for work on roads, 91 percent of whom were black. The results in terms of infrastructure were impressive. By the end of 1915, Georgia had thirteen thousand miles of surfaced roads, more than any other southern state.[24]

North Carolina, which had a decentralized system in which each county determined for itself how to handle its prisoners, adopted road gangs piecemeal. In 1926, forty-eight of North Carolina's one hundred counties, with two-thirds of the state population, maintained chain gangs. Over sixteen hundred of the convicts were black; around eight hundred were white. About half of the sentences, for both races, were under one year.[25]

Unsurprisingly, reports of horrific conditions reminiscent of the lease started to mount. Historian Alex Lichtenstein presented this disturbing account, worth a lengthy quote.

> Muckraking accounts of the chain gang from the 1920s, 1930s, and even late 1940s reveal that convicts continued to labor, eat, and sleep with chains riveted around their ankles. Work was done under the gun from sunup to sundown, shoveling dirt at fourteen shovelfuls a minute. Food was bug infested, rotten, and unvarying; rest was taken in unwashed bedding, often in wheeled cages nine feet wide by twenty feet long containing eighteen beds. Medical treatment and bathing facilities were unsanitary, if available at all. And above all, corporal punishment and outright torture—casual blows from rifle butts or clubs, whipping with a leather strap, confinement in a sweatbox under the southern sun, and hanging from stocks or bars—was meted out for the most insignificant transgressions, particularly to African Americans who were the majority of chain-gang prisoners.[26]

The lease was worse than the chain gang, of course, but only in a few respects. The work was more dangerous in mines and swamps than in open fields, where roads were laid, so the mortality rate for leasing was much higher. And the leasing contractors, assured of a certain number of laborers, were even more indifferent to the health and safety of the inmates than the publicly employed guards. But the working conditions, the physical abuse, and the blatant racism of the chain gang will always be a stain on the history of America's justice system.

6

THE DECLINE OF DEATH

THE DEATH PENALTY was fairly common in the colonial period of American history, but its use has tailed off ever since. From the late nineteenth century on, executions per capita have declined, though there were spikes during crime booms, such as in the early 1930s and the 1970s.

Taking the long view, there has been a historic decline in the use of capital punishment in the United States, along with a search for the least painful way to impose it. This decline can be seen as part of the multi-century movement to abolish corporal (that is, bodily) punishment. Consequently, as we enter the third decade of the twenty-first century, capital punishment has become a near rarity. And when it is imposed, it is carried out by lethal injection, which is far less painful than any previous execution method. There were only 22 executions in 2019, and the annual average in the last five years was 24. Compare these figures to the post-1977 high of 98 executions in 1999 alone, and the twentieth-century peak of 199 executions in 1935. It is telling that two-thirds of the states—thirty-four out of fifty—have abolished the death penalty altogether or have not carried out an execution in at least ten years.[1]

From 1608 to 2002 the United States (and the English colonies of North America) executed an estimated 15,269 persons. However, we can't be sure of the exact number of executions because up to the last 150 years, careful records were not kept.[2] From the numbers researchers have collected, however, we can conclude that the execution rate from colonial America to the current day—the number of executions in light of the size of the population—has declined dramatically. The rate from 1766 through 1785, just before the Constitution was drafted, was a bit under two per 100,000. If this doesn't sound very impressive, compare the rates in subsequent centuries. In the nineteenth century the rate was consistently below 0.4 per 100,000, falling to below 0.2 per 100,000 in the twentieth. In other words, taking population size into account, ten times as many people were put to death in the late eighteenth century as in the twentieth.[3]

What accounts for this dramatic decline? Clearly, attitudes toward capital punishment have changed significantly over the course of American history, from strongly in favor during the colonial period, to significantly scrupled in the current era, with many fluctuations in between. As will be shown in the next chapter, this downturn in executions corresponds to the decline in the use of whippings and other forms of bodily punishments. One explanation for this is a change in sensibilities among Americans, a growing revulsion toward bodily pain and compassion for those compelled to endure it.[4]

Also, especially since 1976, the Supreme Court has mandated procedures in capital cases that have made imposing the penalty considerably more difficult. Trials are much longer and costlier than they had been, and appeals take a decade or even two to complete. Many states and counties do not want to expend limited criminal justice resources in time and money on capital prosecutions. The upshot is that the contemporary punishment for even heinous crimes is far more lenient than it had been. Murderers are seldom executed, and other serious crimes, such as the rape of a child, are no longer legally punishable by death.[5]

In the colonial era, from the seventeenth century to the first half of the eighteenth, there was little serious opposition to capital punishment. It isn't that the colonists were especially cruel or indifferent to human life; rather, there were limited options for dealing with serious crime because the modern prison had not yet been invented. Aside from transporting (exiling) a depraved criminal (which England did in those days, adding to the American population), what could be done with such a person? Public hanging seemed the best answer, as it provided retribution in truly odious cases, deterred others from engaging in similar acts—especially given the public nature of the execution—and afforded an opportunity for salvation in the afterlife for the truly penitent offender.[6]

By the end of the eighteenth century, opposition to the death penalty, led by the influential Benjamin Rush, became a social movement. The first sustained attack on capital punishment was penned by Italian philosopher Cesare Beccaria in 1764. Beccaria's *Essay on Crimes and Punishments* was translated into English and circulated widely in the colonies. Soon people were doubting that mere crimes against property deserved a death sentence. By the 1790s Pennsylvania and New York had established prisons, and the effort to reduce the application of the death penalty crystallized. In 1794, Pennsylvania provided prison sentences for treason, manslaughter, rape, arson, and counterfeiting—all formerly capital crimes. Even murder was modified by dividing it into degrees; only first-degree murder could result in death; second degree murder was punishable by imprisonment alone. Within the next few years, four other states abolished the death penalty for crimes other than murder, and three adopted the degrees approach.[7]

Although southern states also embraced curtailments of capital punishment, such reforms were for whites only. The large slave population (more than half the residents of some southern states) required special restraints to keep them from rebelling, running off, attacking their masters, or destroying their property. Consequently, the southern states passed specific death penalty laws for African Americans for such crimes as burning crops or goods or maiming or bruising whites (South Carolina); preparing or administering medicine (criminalized in Georgia to prevent poisonings); conspiring to rebel, raping a white woman, or setting fire to a house (Maryland). Unsurprisingly, execution rates for blacks far exceeded the rates for southern whites.[8] Nonetheless, slave owners were reluctant to execute bondsmen, as to do so would mean loss of labor and an expensive replacement. To encourage trials for serious crimes by slaves, several southern states established funds to compensate owners if a slave was tried and executed.[9]

After slavery ended, African Americans faced both official and unofficial death penalties, with lynchings outnumbering lawful executions. Before the 1890s southern lynchings were mainly of whites, and in the far West few blacks were ever lynched. But starting in the 1890s, for reasons not entirely clear, lynchings of blacks soared in the South. There were 799 in that decade alone, a peak in American history.[10] Part of the explanation was the economic recession of 1893, creating economic insecurity among poor whites; part was the pot-stirring by openly racist politicians; part was a kind of contagion or copycat behavior, fueled by lurid coverage in the press; and part was a rise in black crime.[11]

In the twentieth century the trend for lynching was steadily downward. In the 1920s there were 206 black victims, 88 in the 1930s. Attitudes had changed, even in the South, where by 1937, 65 percent of those surveyed favored federal criminalization of lynching. By 1940 legal executions had supplanted punishment by mob throughout the United States. While there were occasional lynchings in the 1940s, '50s, and '60s—for example, Emmett Till in 1955, and civil rights volunteers James Chaney, Andrew Goodman, and Michael Schwerner in 1964— they were atypical reminders of our ghastly history.[12]

Lawful execution methods became less harsh and degrading over the course of U.S. history. Hanging predominated for hundreds of years both for legal executions and lynchings (although burning to death was not unknown in the eighteenth century). But hanging could be painful, especially if the executioner was inexperienced. Done wrong, hanging could cause an agonizingly slow strangulation death, and apparently this was not an uncommon outcome.[13]

In the colonial era and the first two decades of the nineteenth century hangings were public. The idea was to unite the community in a solemn justice ritual. But as the witnessing crowds turned rowdy states moved executions out of public locations, usually into jail yards. Even before crowds became unruly the growing middle class in the United States had become more sensitive to the suffering of others and more contemptuous of those who enjoyed watching the infliction of pain. By the 1830s virtually all northern states had moved hangings into the jail yard, and though southern states lagged—after all, they countenanced public lynchings—by century's end nearly all lawful executions were held out of public view.[14]

The next significant development was the search for a less painful method of executing. In the 1880s the latest technology—electricity—was increasingly touted as the modern way to do death. A New York State commission compared electrocution to the alternatives and concluded that it was relatively fast, painless, certain, clean, and cheap. The leading electricity experts of the day, George Westinghouse, Thomas Edison, and Nikola Tesla, were involved one way or another in the development of an electric chair. The first attempt to use such a device—on William Kemmler, who had murdered his girlfriend—was bungled, and the execution, held in 1890 at Auburn Prison, was gruesome to watch. Nevertheless, the U.S. Supreme Court rebuffed a legal challenge to electrocution and it was used again in New York shortly after the Kemmler fiasco, this time with success. By 1913, fourteen states had joined New York in adopting the chair. Although doctors assured the public that the condemned felt no pain, electrocution certainly looked painful, and the search for a better method continued.[15]

Asphyxiation by lethal gas was the next technological advance, with eleven western and southern states adopting it in the 1930s. Nevada had been the first, in 1921. Nevada had switched to gas from the firing squad, used (in Nevada and Utah) because of the Mormon demand for atonement by blood. But death by poison gas also had problems. First, it required a sealed chamber for the gas to work, yet there was danger to spectators due to leakage. In addition, opponents thought, in death penalty historian Stuart Banner's words, there was "something sinister, something creepy" about executing someone sealed into a small enclosed space that he alone occupied. The final negative was that gas executions were sometimes painful, as the chemicals didn't always work as fast as they were supposed to. Ultimately, the gas chamber, like the electric chair, was replaced by lethal injection.[16]

By the 1970s lethal injection was adopted as the most efficient and least painful means of executing. Oklahoma and Texas were the first states to use the needle, in 1977, a year after the Supreme Court sanctioned its use. Before long, every death sentence was carried out this way. The preferred procedure is a three-drug cocktail of Pentathol, a fast-acting sedative to induce coma-like sleep; followed by pancuronium bromide, which paralyzes the diaphragm, stopping respiration; and potassium chloride, which induces cardiac arrest. The Supreme Court approved this method, though the late Justice Ruth Bader Ginsburg dissented on the grounds that Kentucky, the state involved, didn't adequately examine the condemned man to see if the Pentathol had worked.[17]

* * *

Following World War II, efforts to abolish the death penalty intensi-fied. Perhaps all the killing during the war reinforced efforts to abolish death as a punishment. The development of the civil rights movement also may have played a role since a disproportionate number of capital defendants were African Americans. However, high black murder rates with overwhelmingly black victims blunted the argument that capital punishment was administered in a racially biased manner.[18]

While violent crime rates in the 1950s and early 1960s were low, the public appeared willing to countenance fewer capital sentences, and the numbers declined rather dramatically. Executions plummeted over 90 percent, from 105 in 1951 to only 7 in 1965.[19]

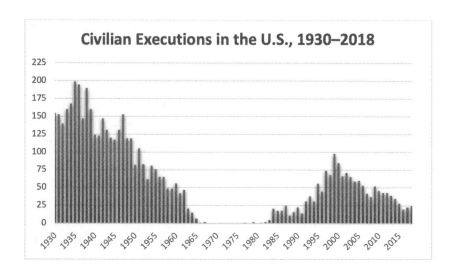

By the end of the 1960s, however, widespread rioting and violent crime had reached epic heights, and the demand for law and order became a political mantra. Given this backdrop, the country was stunned and disturbed when in 1972 the Supreme Court, in *Furman v. Georgia*, declared the death penalty to be unconstitutionally cruel and unusual punishment. However, a close look at the ruling revealed that only two of the nine justices favored absolute abolition, whereas seven thought that the laws could pass constitutional muster if redrawn. The defect in the laws, the latter bloc of judges reasoned, was that they were applied erratically; some heinous murderers were executed, while others were only imprisoned. Likewise, some less odious killings led to a death sentence. Of course, the same inconsistencies could be found with every crime; no offense is punished in a perfectly consistent way in terms of the degree of reprehensibility. Nonetheless, the justices said, revealing their own arbitrariness, "death is different."[20]

For an eleven-year period, 1968 to 1978, only one death sentence was carried out in the United States. Given the horrific crime situation, the public was eager to reinstate the death penalty, and following *Furman* thirty-five states rewrote their capital punishment laws. But it wasn't clear how state laws could resolve the problem of inconsistent application of death sentences raised in the *Furman* case. Georgia hit upon the answer: limit the penalty to the worst of the worst, that is, to "aggravated" murders that aren't outweighed by so-called mitigating circumstances. Only these worst cases would be death-eligible; less reprehensible murders could only be punished by imprisonment, usually life without parole. This formula was upheld in *Gregg v. Georgia* (1976), and the Georgia law became a model for the nation.

Although the Court stood by its decision in *Gregg*, it really didn't solve the inconsistency problem. There was nothing to stop a prosecutor from accepting a plea of guilty, even in a heinous case, and agreeing to a prison sentence. Nor could a prosecutor be prevented from seeking death in a murder that, while "aggravated," might also offer compelling mitigation, such as a youthful defendant without an extensive criminal record.

But the biggest problem with *Gregg*, from the standpoint of those favoring the death penalty, was the expense required to carry it out. The Georgia law divided capital trials into two parts to permit evidence of aggravation and mitigation to be presented without prejudicing the jury's decision on guilt. The effect was a very long and expensive trial, almost two trials in one. And if the lengthy trial wasn't bad enough, every death sentence would have to be followed by a protracted and costly appeals process. In 2018 it was taking nearly twenty years to complete the appeals.[21]

Given the expense, and the intensity of feelings among opponents of the death penalty, it is not clear that capital punishment will continue to be imposed in the United States, except perhaps in a handful of cases. This situation could change, of course, especially if there is another massive crime wave, as there had been in the late 1960s to the mid-1990s. But as things now stand, murderers are likely to receive the more lenient punishment of a lengthy prison sentence.[22]

7

THE FAILURE OF LENIENCY

FROM THE 1930s TO THE LATE 1960s, when a twenty-five-year crime boom demolished their vision, penal reformers dominated the criminal justice system. Because each state managed (and to this day controls) its own prisons the adoption of rehabilitation-oriented policies was uneven. States like New York and California were in the vanguard, while the Deep South held up the rear. But all states were affected by the drive for more lenient policies: prisoner classification, an end to corporal punishment and forced labor, more amenities, recreational activities, psychological interventions, various educational and vocational programs, and "community corrections," meaning probation instead of prison and parole instead of full-term sentences. In fact, many of these leniencies became legal mandates, imposed by activist courts that developed novel and sweeping interpretations of laws long dormant. A prisoners' rights movement, which gathered steam in the 1960s, turned out to be reformism's last hurrah—until the current-day decarceration efforts.

Despite the reforms, or maybe because of them—raised expectations unsatisfied serve as a major catalyst for revolts—inmates rioted in the late 1920s, the early 1950s, and especially in the 1960s and early 1970s. Not only did they revolt when incarcerated, they continued to reoffended in large numbers once released. Such signs of the failure of reformism were obvious. But after each spate of prison disturbances, the response was the same: there wasn't enough support, not enough money, or, there was too much emphasis on security, on preventing escapes, not enough on reforming the offender, reintegrating him back into society. So, after the violence and the lockdowns came new reforms, following which the cycle started all over again.

A striking example of this is the aftermath of the 1971 riot at Attica prison in New York, one of the most highly publicized prisoner revolts in American history. It left twenty-nine prisoners and ten of their hostages dead. In the very next legislative session, in 1972, eight bills to improve prison conditions were passed by the state legislature, and Governor Nelson Rockefeller approved $12 million in new funds for corrections. In fact, after Attica there were pro-prisoner changes across the country throughout the 1970s.[1]

This cycle of reform-revolt-more reform climaxed during the great crime tsunami, perhaps the biggest violent crime wave in American history, which ran from the end of the 1960s to the middle of the 1990s.[2] This crime boom brought the reform movement to a screeching halt—but it didn't eliminate the leniencies.

* * *

One of the major and lasting reforms of the Progressive Era was the classification of prisoners. It grew out of a psychological explanation for crime, popular in the early decades of the twentieth century. Offenders were damaged mentally, it was thought, and at least some could be treated and therefore rehabilitated through psychological counseling.

This required individualized examination of each new inmate and differentiation—classification—according to their amenability to improvement. By 1926, sixty-seven prisons employed psychiatrists and forty-five employed psychologists—enough to classify, but not to treat all or even most of the inmates. This morphed into a sorting of prisoners based on the seriousness of their crimes and their criminal histories, which eventually turned into separate high-security cell blocks or prisons for the hardened and dangerous versus less secure facilities for young first-offenders whose crimes were not as reprehensible. Soon every state had minimum-, medium-, and maximum-security facilities.[3]

Classification benefited the administrators by enabling them to impose more stringent limitations on the most dangerous inmates while sparing the less troublesome. It also enabled them to transfer prisoners to the more restrictive cell blocks or even separate prisons if they became obstreperous, a deterrence to rules violations. But classification aided prisoners too, as it protected the less dangerous and more vulnerable from being preyed upon by the more vicious. (Parchman is an object lesson in the failure to classify. See pages 41-44.)

There also were experiments in classification that aimed at real rehabilitation, such as the Norfolk Prison Colony in Massachusetts, in operation as an experimental institution from 1927 to 1934. Run by Howard Gill, an efficiency expert and Harvard Business School graduate, Norfolk classified prisoners into five categories, identified by the acronym "SCAMP":

SITUATIONAL (occasional offenders who will reform once the causal situation is eliminated)

CUSTODIAL (incapable of treatment due to mature age or mental insufficiency; the hardened criminal)

ASOCIAL (anti-social attitudes; gangsters, racketeers)

MEDICAL (resorted to crime due to physical afflictions preventing success in the legitimate world)

PERSONALITY CASES (crime due to psychotic or neurotic personality)

This classification was not designed for segregating prisoners by dangerousness. Rather, it was a therapeutic classification, devised to facilitate rehabilitation through different treatments. Thus, the situational offender required the techniques applied by the social worker; the asocial required the methods of the educator; the medical, a physician; the personality, a psychiatrist. The custodial, impervious to reform, required guarding.[4]

It wasn't long before the Norfolk experiment failed. The SCAMP categories were inadequate guides to treatment, and the prisoners were handled differently in terms of housing and privileges based on their cooperativeness with the programs. Some of the inmates resented the different treatment and refused to play the game. Gill had to resort to punishments, such as solitary confinement, to treat the recalcitrants. There were other setbacks as well. Program resources were always insufficient; no surprise given that this was the depths of the Great Depression. As more and more prisoners were sent to Norfolk, managing them grew increasingly problematic. After some escapes the media started running exposés of Norfolk's problems. By 1934 Gill was out and the experiment was over. Norfolk became just another prison. But the concept of classification—not to cure but to secure convicts—became institutionalized.[5]

* * *

Corporal punishment was a mainstay of the American penal system for over three hundred years, from its founding in the seventeenth century through the first half of the twentieth. But increased public revulsion over the imposition of pain as a punishment diminished its use, and it was eventually replaced by solitary confinement.[6] Of course, long-term solitary in a dark, unventilated cell, with minimal food (the proverbial bread and water) and no human contact, is uniquely painful, though in a different way than the whip. While solitary is still used today, it is far more limited than the cruelties of the 1920s and 1930s. In the late 1920s, for example, Wyoming used pitch-black underground cells. Ohio, in 1926, made inmates stand in a close-fitting steel cage eight or more hours a day. Joliet Prison, in Illinois, confined prisoners in solitary for one to seven days, handcuffed to a cell door for twelve hours, and fed only four ounces of bread and one quart of water daily. Nevada's solitary cells were infested with mice and snakes.[7]

Early in the twentieth century, most states outlawed corporal punishment as a sentence for crime. Delaware was the last state to maintain a whipping post, and it didn't abolish corporal punishment for crimes until 1972. However, unofficial corporal punishments to discipline inmates were common throughout the United States up to World War II. In the South, Arkansas, Texas, Florida, and Louisiana routinely lashed convicts. After the war, and especially as a result of the prisoners' rights movement, which began in the 1960s, everything changed.[8]

By the end of the 1960s, corporal punishment as discipline had become an anachronism. As of 1968, only two states, Arkansas and Mississippi, continued to discipline prisoners with a whip or strap. But not for long. Federal courts struck down such practices on the grounds that they violated the cruel and unusual punishments clause of the Constitution. In the Arkansas case, Judge Harry Blackmun (later elevated to the U.S. Supreme Court) wrote "that the use of the strap in the penitentiaries of Arkansas is punishment which, in this last third of the 20th century, runs afoul of the Eighth Amendment; [and furthermore] that the strap's use, irrespective of any precautionary conditions which may be imposed, offends contemporary concepts of decency and human dignity and precepts of civilization which we profess to possess."[9]

* * *

Forced labor was another longstanding feature of the American justice

THE FAILURE OF LENIENCY

system. In fact, it was considered essential to rehabilitation when penitentiaries were invented at the end of the eighteenth century. Done right, it
could have been a vehicle for vocational training; but it was seldom done
right. Inmate labor also was seen as a way to offset the expense of building
and maintaining prisons. Nor was it a constitutional problem since the
Thirteenth Amendment, which prohibited slavery, expressly permitted
"involuntary servitude . . . as a punishment for crime."[10]

But there were two big difficulties with forced labor as punishment.
First, there were the horrors of the convict lease and its successors, the road
gang and the penal farm. (See chapter 5.) Black inmates were abused and
died at shockingly high rates while under the control of businessmen or
their employees who considered them little more than expendable labor.
Matters improved, but only somewhat, when the state or county took
over and built roads with chain gangs. A potentially better solution, at
least in the South, where the weather was mild year-round, was the penal
farm, where inmates raised crops, such as cotton, for sale. But given the
Jim Crow practices of the first half of the twentieth century, the black
prisoners got the short end of the stick once again, and it took federal
court intervention (in the 1960s) to halt the farms' worst features.[11]

Then there was the competition-with-free-labor problem. In the late
nineteenth century, the states above the Mason-Dixon line contracted
with private manufacturers to use convicts to produce goods for sale
on the open market by bringing raw materials, machinery, and supervisors into the prison. As might be expected, free laborers and businesses
complained bitterly about the unfair competition, and free workers
even organized strikes in protest. While New York abolished the contract system in 1894, it remained popular in other states through the
1920s. Historian David Rothman reports that in 1923, 40 percent of
all prison-made goods were made under this system, and 60 percent of
all prison-made goods were sold on the open market.

That didn't last long. Under pressure from free labor and industry,
Congress passed the Hawes-Cooper Act in 1929, enabling states to strip
goods produced in out-of-state prisons of their interstate commerce

protection. In other words, a state could tax or keep out altogether goods made in the prisons of other states. Hawes-Cooper and allied laws passed in the 1930s crippled prison labor. "By 1932 only 16 percent of all inmates worked for private contractors," Rothman found, "and by 1940 the practice practically disappeared." Of course, 1932 was the nadir of the Great Depression, when jobs were scarce and production was low across the entire economy. Still, the work situation in the prisons in the 1930s was especially dire: in forty-seven of eighty-five state prisons over 50 percent were unemployed; in another nineteen prisons over 40 percent were.[12]

World War II inspired patriotism among prison inmates and led to a relaxation of restraints on prison industries. President Franklin D. Roosevelt issued an executive order in 1942 eliminating legal barriers to war contracts with prisons. This ended idleness for two years and even meant decent earnings for some inmates. Unfortunately, when the war contracts terminated, so did most prison industry.[13]

When it came to manufacturing, all that remained for prisons was the state-use system, where products such as license plates or inmate clothes—articles used by state governments—could be produced, or public works projects could be undertaken. But state use simply didn't provide enough work to employ large numbers of inmates.[14]

The decline of prison labor presented corrections administrators with a new problem, a problem without a good solution—forced idleness. You know things are bad when a former Parchman inmate waxes nostalgic over Black Annie, hand-picked cotton, and dawn-to-dusk labor in the fields. Horace Carter, an inmate for almost fifty years, told historian David Oshinsky that what was missing now (after federal courts put an end to the old system) was "the feeling that work counted for something." "Awful bad as it was in most camps, that [work] kept us tired and kept us together and made me feel better inside."[15]

* * *

By the 1950s Progressives had radically reduced both forced labor and corporal punishment and substituted freedom of the yard, sports, movies, music, mail, and visits. Correctional institutions managed by professional administrators replaced the "big houses" run by political appointees. But the number of inmates was steadily increasing, and the trend was to pack 'em in even if it meant two men in a cell designed for one. Prison populations rose 27 percent in the 1950s.[16]

Overcrowding seems to have been the principal reason for a dozen prison riots in the early 1950s, though news of especially brutal incidents, such as floggings in Louisiana, helped create solidarity among inmates. There were uprisings in the New Jersey state prison in Trenton; at the huge facility in Jackson, Michigan; in Concord, Massachusetts; at a road camp in Georgia; in Columbus, Ohio; in the Western Penitentiary (near Pittsburgh); and even at what was then considered the beacon of progressivism, Soledad Prison in California. These rebellions often led to administrative reforms, including additional facilities, improved classification of prisoners, and some experimental rehabilitation programs.

But clearly, since riots occurred in Progressive systems as often as in regressive ones, rehabilitation programs weren't reducing prisoner dissatisfaction. As prison historian Blake McKelvey put it, "The prison riots and other disturbances revealed the widespread failure of the reformatory objective."[17]

Riots aside, the conclusion that rehabilitation programs weren't reforming prisoners and preventing reoffending was borne out by a famous review by sociologist Robert Martinson of hundreds of rehabilitation studies. The studies evaluated programs dating from the 1950s through the 1960s. "What Works?" was the title of Martinson's article, and the answer seemed to be "Nothing." He concluded that the data generated by the research,

> involving over two hundred studies and hundreds of thousands of individuals as they do, are the best available and give us very little reason to hope that we have in fact found a sure way of reducing recidivism through rehabilitation. This is not to say that we found no instances of success or partial success; it is only to say that these

instances have been isolated, producing no clear pattern to indicate the efficacy of any particular method of treatment.[18]

Even leftist activists of the day condemned the reform-oriented approach to the criminal justice system. The *Struggle for Justice* report, issued by the Quakers, denied that prison treatment programs were effective and rejected that hallmark of progressivism, indeterminate sentencing. Instead, they endorsed short, fixed sentences for repeat offenders, without regard to the unique characteristics of the individual.[19]

***

Riots flared anew in the late 1960s, but this time the cause was different. The civil rights movement and the Vietnam War generated an atmosphere of rebellion in the nation, and radical views became popular among the increasing number of young minorities in prison. (Nationwide, in 1970, prisons were nearly 40 percent nonwhite—triple the proportion of the nonwhite population of the country.[20]) Resentful attitudes and mistrust and animosity toward white prison guards and administrators were fostered by militant African American organizations, especially the Black Panthers and Black Muslims. In the case of the Muslims, also known as the Nation of Islam, constitutional guarantees of religious freedom made it difficult for administrators to suppress activities in the prisons.[21] Some of the black inmates began to see themselves as political prisoners, and riots were viewed as revolutionary acts. In 1969 alone there were thirty-nine prison disturbances; fifty-nine more occurred in 1970. Two dozen of these uprisings were planned, not spontaneous. Hostages were taken in twenty-five incidents, and there were five deaths.[22]

The most notorious of the riots, and one of the bloodiest, occurred in 1971 at New York's Attica Correctional Facility. Thirty-nine people—ten hostages and 29 inmates—were shot to death by state troopers in an effort to retake the prison after 1,281 inmates seized forty guards, four cellblocks, and all the facility's yards and tunnels. The shooting took place after four days of tense negotiations had stalled over the inmates' demands for complete amnesty.[23]

Before the shocking end to the Attica rebellion, there had been several precipitating incidents. In 1970 there were upheavals in New York City's jails, and numerous inmates were sent upstate to Attica, where they added to the crowded conditions. In an uprising at the old Auburn prison that same year, around fifty corrections officers were taken hostage; four were brutally beaten. Six of the Auburn instigators were transferred to Attica and kept in segregation there for six months.[24]

The shooting death of George Jackson in California's San Quentin Prison was another triggering event. Jackson, an admirer of black militants Eldridge Cleaver and Malcolm X, had become a hero to prisoners of color. After Jackson was charged with the murder of a white guard, a support drive that included several California state legislators was mounted. Meanwhile, George's younger brother, Jonathan, raided the Marin County Courthouse and kidnapped a judge and several jurors. He demanded George's release and in the ensuing shootout he and two companions died along with the judge. George, with inmate help, then seized part of San Quentin and took six guards hostage, killing four. George was shot to death as he fled across the yard. Needless to say, the events involving the Jackson brothers received enormous media attention and further stoked the anger of black prisoners nationwide.[25]

The day after Jackson's death, Attica inmates donned black armbands and staged a silent protest at mealtime. A few weeks later, some incidents between prisoners and guards culminated in a full-fledged rebellion and the hostage-taking of forty corrections officers. Corrections commissioner Russell Oswald, newly appointed to his position, agreed to negotiate with inmate leaders in the hope of a peaceful resolution. The negotiations were covered by the media and involved state politicians, journalists, and radical attorneys such as William Kunstler, along with a self-selected group of prison leaders, all minorities.

After four days of tense negotiations, a twenty-eight-point agreement was reached on a range of reforms, including improvements in food and medical care, more religious and political freedom, legal assistance for prisoners, and changes in parole procedures. But the inmates rejected the agreement because it didn't include criminal amnesty, which Oswald felt he had no authority to grant. New York's governor, Nelson Rockefeller, was adamant that he could not legally grant amnesty and said he wouldn't grant it in any event "because it would undermine the very essence of our free society—the fair and impartial application of the law." On the fifth day after the takeover, Oswald, with Rockefeller's approval, ordered the reclaiming of Attica by force. Although rumors stated that the convicts had killed the hostages—and two surviving guards had slash wounds on their necks requiring fifty-two and thirty stitches, respectively—the medical examiner's report concluded that all ten of the dead hostages had been killed by police bullets.[26]

The fact is, Attica as a prison was no worse than the five other maximum-security facilities in New York in 1971. The conditions were horrible, as one would expect, but hardly cruel and unusual. Ironically, Commissioner Oswald, the man who ordered the assault on Attica, was sympathetic to the prisoners, had been preparing reforms before the takeover, and had agreed to all of the inmate demands save criminal amnesty. But even had the reforms been enacted, the uprising probably would have occurred anyway because the real explanation for it was the new militancy of the minority prisoners. Improved conditions would not have assuaged the radical inmates who grossly exaggerated the problems of New York's prisons, which they called "concentration camps."[27]

* * *

Around the same time as Attica, and undoubtedly propelled by sympathy for black inmates, a prisoners' rights movement was making significant headway in the federal courts. The movement was an offshoot of the drive for African American civil rights. They were related in two ways. First, as already noted, there were increasing numbers of African Americans incarcerated and segregated in the prisons, and their treatment in the southern penal systems was abominable.[28] So, although harsh treatment, not racial segregation, was the big problem with American prisons, segregation in prisons couldn't be reconciled with the cases abolishing the Jim Crow system. Though separation by race probably inhibited interracial violence among white and minority inmates, segregation had to go.[29]

The civil rights movement advanced prisoners' rights in a second way. It created a new generation of legal activists, who used their positions on the bench to advance reforms in several fields, including criminal justice. The result was a series of cases ordering significantly improved conditions in prisons, setting the stage for today's much more lenient prison system.[30]

The first major case was *Holt v. Sarver*, which declared the entire Arkansas farm prison operation to be cruel and unusual punishment.[31] Arkansas's farm was a lot like Mississippi's Parchman (see chapter 5), only perhaps worse in that the trusties ran the entire prison, corrupting virtually every activity affecting the lives of the other inmates. As the court described, trusties took bribes and extorted money from inmates; smuggled contraband weapons, liquor, and drugs into the facility; and ran various rackets, forcing the other inmates to pay them exorbitant tribute for such things as coffee, or even medical care. "For the ordinary convict," declared the court, "a sentence to the Arkansas Penitentiary today amounts to a banishment from civilized society to a dark and evil world completely alien to the free world, a world that is administered by criminals under unwritten rules and customs completely foreign to free world culture."[32]

By the 1970s that dark and evil world was ending. Parchman's prime land was leased to local growers; Arkansas hired civilian guards; Texas eliminated its "building tenders" (trusties) and doubled its guard force.[33] The prison farms began to look like northern prisons, with bored, resentful, overwhelmingly black inmates guarded by bored, resentful, overwhelmingly black (and poorly paid) corrections officers. The court rulings improved conditions, dramatically in some cases, but they didn't reduce inmate uprisings, nor did they prevent new crimes once the prisoners were released.

The prisoners' rights decisions changed attitudes and power relationships within the prisons. Starting in the 1970s the guards became fearful and the inmates emboldened. Historian Robert Perkinson described the Texas system after *Ruiz v. Estelle* (1980) eliminated its building tender system.[34]

> "It's changed because you can't put that boot in their ass," explained a
> veteran [guard]. "Ain't no fear no more." Many convicts relished the
> change. While new boots [officers] hesitated, confused by the limits
> on their authority, convicts started to stand up straight, their resolve
> stiffened by victories in court. Once obsequious, prisoners turned
> obstreperous. "Quit harassing me you old country punk," went a
> typical retort. "Fuck all you whores, you can't tell me what to do
> anymore." . . . Terror, once the companion of inmates, began creeping
> into the guard force. "I've been struck several times, been bitten by
> inmates," reported one officer. "Some of them, I'm afraid of. I'm
> afraid to say something to them because I know what I'm going to get.

Once the rights genie was unleashed, court decisions covered a remarkable range of subjects affecting prisoners. Not all of the decisions expanded prisoner rights, and many Supreme Court rulings only set forth general rules for lower courts to apply in subsequent cases. But though it would go too far to say that the judges were running America's prisons, from the 1970s on it became clear that inmates now had a legal forum to challenge prison policies and the advantage of numerous advocacy organizations, from the ACLU (American Civil Liberties Union) to the NAACP, to pay for their lawyers.[35]

Here's a chronological list of some of the major United States Supreme Court cases establishing prisoner rights. The list is not comprehensive, nor does it include the many cases decided by the lower federal courts or state tribunals. But it gives a taste of the breadth of the penological issues addressed by the judiciary.

THE FAILURE OF LENIENCY

- *Cooper v. Pate*, 378 U.S. 546 (1964): Black Muslim prisoners can challenge in federal court prison policies that prevent receipt of religious publications.

- *Younger v. Gilmore*, 404 U.S. 15 (1971): prisoners are entitled to reasonable access to a law library or to persons trained in the law.

- *Cruz v. Beto*, 405 U.S. 319 (1972): a prisoner is entitled to the same right to pursue his Buddhist faith as inmates adhering to more conventional religions.

- *Morrisey v. Brewer*, 408 U.S. 471 (1972): a hearing before a neutral and detached body, such as a parole board, is required to determine the facts related to the revocation of parole.

- *Gagnon v. Scarpelli*, 411 U.S. 778 (1973): a probationer's sentence can only be revoked after a preliminary and a final revocation hearing.

- *Procunier v. Martinez*, 416 U.S. 396 (1974): Invalidating state prison mail censorship regulations.

- *Wolff v. McDonnell*, 418 U.S. 539 (1974): a prisoner facing a disciplinary proceeding has the right to advance written notice of the claimed violation and a written statement of the facts in support of the claim. He also should be allowed to call witnesses and present documentary evidence in his defense.

- *Estelle v. Gamble*, 429 U.S. 97 (1976): deliberate indifference to a prisoner's serious medical needs can constitute cruel and unusual punishment.

- *Bell v. Wolfish*, 441 U.S. 520 (1979): courts may consider the constitutionality of conditions in federal short-term detention facilities, mainly involving inmates awaiting trial.

- *Superintendent v. Hill*, 472 U.S. 445 (1985): revocation of good time credits requires at least "some evidence" in support of the decision.

- *Turner v. Safely*, 482 U.S. 78 (1987): a regulation permitting an inmate to marry only with the prison superintendent's permission is unconstitutional

- *Johnson v. California*, 543 U.S. 499 (2005): racial segregation for sixty days of new or transferred prisoners in order to prevent racial gang violence must be judged by the strictest legal test for violation of the equal protection clause of the Fourteenth Amendment.

- *Wilkinson v. Austin*, 545 U.S. 209 (2005): prisoners may challenge in federal court the process used to determine placement in a supermax facility with restrictions akin to solitary confinement, but the procedures adopted by Ohio provide due process of law.

* * *

By the 1970s the American prison system had undergone a major transformation. The days of forced labor, of beatings and torture, and of open racism were over, replaced by more amenities, recreational activities, and more outright release to probation and parole. With litigation and adverse media coverage raising the possibility of dismissal, loss of pension and even criminal prosecution of correctional personnel, the guards were put on the defensive and the prisoners knew it. Some states contracted out their prison systems to private companies to save money. Some built supermax prisons to isolate violent gang members in medium-to-long-term solitary confinement, one of the few remaining sanctions that could nowadays be imposed on an inmate. But supermax aside, this was, in President George H. W. Bush's aphorism, a kinder and gentler prison system.

Crime rose by leaps and bounds starting in the late 1960s, and in the wake of massive numbers of recidivists, confidence in rehabilitation programs drained away. "Nothing works" became the new mantra, feeding a penology focused on incapacitation. After all, if we can't reform 'em, the attitude was, at least we could take 'em out of circulation.

Critics on the left grumbled that the prisons had become human warehouses, simply holding inmates without improving them before release. Given the enormous recidivism figures, they had a good point. Critics on the right bemoaned the enormous expense associated with the steady expansion of the criminal justice system to meet the escalating crime problem. They too were right. But no one had a good answer to these objections, and no one has one now either *because there is currently no satisfactory replacement for the prison.*

At the end of this book, I recommend some technological alternatives. As I'll show, electronic monitoring is cheaper and more effective than prisons or community corrections without such technologies—and the science is bound to improve. But we should have no illusions. While such technological advances may address the public safety question, they cannot meet the punitive or retributive aims of the criminal justice system. And retribution—justice—will always be at the heart of any criminal justice system. Heinous crime, serious crime, will still have to be punished, and no one has come up with a better penalty (aside from death for the very worst) than isolation from society.

PART TWO

THE AGE OF LENIENCY

8

THE BUILDUP

TO FULLY UNDERSTAND PUNISHMENT, one must examine crime. Contrary to some analyses (discussed later), crime and punishment are linked. Despite some delays or lags, there is a strong correlation between the two. As a general rule, the more crime, the more punishment, and vice versa. The great buildup of the criminal justice system, including so-called mass incarceration, cannot be understood without examining the crime tsunami that preceded it.

In the late 1960s, just as prisons were becoming less cruel than they had been in all of American history, a titanic crime wave struck the United States with the force of a tsunami. Violent crime—including murder, rape, robbery, and assault—climbed higher and higher each year, terrifying the public. Except for a slight dip in the early 1980s, the escalation was relentless and seemingly unstoppable. The crime tsunami went on for nearly three decades. From the low point in 1961—158 violent crimes for every 100,000 Americans—to the high point in 1991—an eye-popping 758 violent crimes per 100,000—the rise was an astonishing 380 percent.[1]

The public was stricken with fear. In 1972, four out of ten Americans told Gallup pollsters they were afraid to walk alone in their communities at night. Among African Americans, the poor, the elderly, and big-city dwellers, the figure was one out of two.[2] The response was predictable and totally justifiable: beef up the criminal justice system, the public demanded; make it more punitive; get the criminals off the streets. The politicians had to respond, and ultimately, they did.

Decades later, by the 2000s, with crime finally in decline, some writers revised history to suit their new extreme decarceration agenda. These decarcerationists claimed, with little justification, that crime anxiety was just a construct of conservative politicians who "shaped public attitudes" in order "to heighten opposition to the civil rights movement." But public opinion expert Peter Enns demolished this contention, demonstrating persuasively that the reverse was true: a terrified public had pushed a law-and-order agenda *before* the politicians adopted it.[3] Some scholars went further still, denying that a crime wave ever occurred, or downplaying it out of dishonesty or ignorance. I'll offer some shocking examples in the next chapter.

Contrary to the decarceration lobby, the public's fears were fully warranted by the enormous rise in crime. The crime tsunami was not some media-generated moral panic or a by-product of fake statistics; nor was it a Republican plot to undo civil rights or the war on poverty. More Americans were murdered in the crime boom than perished in World War II, the Korean War, the Vietnam War, and the conflicts in Iraq and Afghanistan *combined*. Between 1970 and 1995, a staggering 540,019 Americans were slain. War fatalities totaled 507,340. And if we compare the war-wounded to those injured in criminal assaults, the toll of the crime tsunami is even more shocking. Fewer than one million service personnel suffered nonfatal injuries in the foreign conflicts just named, whereas *2.2 million Americans per year* were injured by violent crime. Over 6 million of the assault injuries, 1973 to 1991, were considered serious, as they involved gunshot or knife wounds, broken bones, loss of consciousness, dislodged teeth, and internal damage. Many crime victims required hospitalizations lasting two days or more. And these losses do not address the financial costs, which ran into the billions, and which usually had to be borne by the victims. The crime tsunami was a war on the American civilian population.[4]

In the late 1960s and early 1970s, the rise in crime was accompanied by hundreds of protests against the war in Vietnam and demonstrations for black civil rights, many of which were extremely violent. The year 1965 marked the first of several long, hot summers as African Americans rampaged in city after city. Historians Stephan and Abigail Thernstrom tallied 329 riots in 257 cities between 1964 and 1968. Economists William Collins and Robert Margo uncovered an even greater number—a shocking 752 racial disorders from 1964 to 1971. By an objective measure of severity, 130 of the 752 riots were considered "major" and 37 were labeled "massive" in destructiveness.[5] Not only was there great loss of life and property, but some cities never really recovered. Newark, New Jersey, a striking example, saw serious long-term economic erosion as whites and middle-class blacks fled the downtown for safer suburbs.[6] The riots, with their wanton looting and destruction of property, added to the toll of crime and heightened public terror.

Despite the rise in crime—or maybe because it was so sudden and massive—the criminal justice system was caught flatfooted and punishments diminished just when they should have been increasing. This is the first of those lags between crime and punishment that I mentioned earlier.

Consider the number of people going to prison for serious crimes. In 1960, for every one thousand arrests for a serious offense 299 people were committed to prison. In 1965 only 261 were imprisoned. And by 1970, when crime and violent disorders were raging, a mere 170 per thousand went to prison, a decadal drop of 43 percent.[7]

Worse still, as crime increased, the police were making fewer, not more, arrests. Take robbery, for instance, the quintessential crime of the period. In 1950 and 1960, around four in ten reported cases were cleared by police, which is not a very high rate to begin with. But by 1970 that rate had declined to under three in ten.[8]

When they were unfortunate enough to be caught, convicted, and imprisoned for their crimes, offenders found that the crime wave was working in their favor: they spent less time behind bars. Staying with the robbery example: in the 1950s and 1960s robbers served a median thirty-four to thirty-seven months (about three years) in prison. By the 1970s and 1980s, prison time for robbery was down to twenty-five months, just over two years.[9]

Did this caving of the criminal justice system serve as an incentive to even more crime? Did it accelerate crime rates in the 1970s and beyond? It's hard to prove this, since one would have to control for every significant factor that could have been responsible for the crime boom, such as the size of the young male population, the strength of police forces, the availability of drugs and guns, and so on. But the inference that a flabby justice system encouraged more crime seems intuitively obvious. After all, analysts demonstrated that the punitiveness eventually adopted ultimately reduced crime rates, so why wouldn't the opposite also be true: that criminal justice flabbiness generated more crime? An observer who wants to be especially cautious could at least say that the weakened criminal justice system did little to stem the rising tide of crime and violence.[10]

* * *

Gradually, but steadily, the criminal justice system was strengthened and more criminals were apprehended and punished. During the 1970s imprisonment rates climbed significantly: up 41 percent by 1980, another 114 percent one decade later.[11] More and more offenders were being incarcerated, and many of them were kept behind bars longer. Rates of imprisonment climbed to new heights, as the accompanying graph shows.

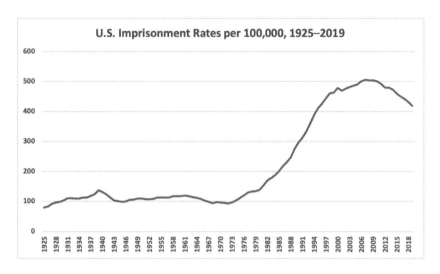

U.S. Imprisonment Rates per 100,000, 1925–2019

Sourcebook of Criminal Justice Statistics Online, table 6.28.2010, http://www.albany.edu/sourcebook/pdf/t6282010.pdf. U.S. Department of Justice, Bureau of Justice Statistics, *Prisoners in 2019* (2020), table 5.

A careful look at the next graph, which plots violent crime and imprisonment rates, reveals the two lags or delays that are integral to my analysis. First, when crime began its meteoric rise in the late 1960s imprisonment remained low. Incarceration started its climb nearly one decade later in the mid-1970s.

The second lag occurred in the mid-1990s, when the crime tsunami finally began to roll back but incarceration was reaching new heights. This lag, between declining crime and elevated imprisonment rates, fed the great anti-incarceration crusade. By this point, the first and far more destructive late 1960s lag was conveniently forgotten, or denied altogether. I'll return to this point in the next chapter.

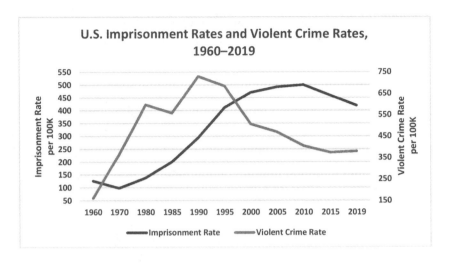

U.S. Imprisonment Rates and Violent Crime Rates, 1960–2019

1960–1990: r = 0.8735; r² = 0.7631

1960–2019: r = 0.12937; r² = 0.01674

A NOTE ON THE STATISTICS

Criminologists and other social scientists use statistical methods to show relationships between factors (or variables). This chart provides an illustration. It depicts the relationship between imprisonment rates and violent crime rates, that is, whether they rise or fall at the same time and to the same extent. The strength of the relationship is indicated by the value of r. The closer r is to 1 (or –1), the stronger the relationship; the closer r is to zero, the weaker is the association. (–1 indicates a negative correlation: as one variable rises, the other falls. The chart suggests that this occurred from 1995 to 2010.)

From 1960 to 1990, r was estimated as .8735, indicating that the relationship was very strong and positive. Measured from 1960 to 2019, estimated r fell to .12937, indicating that the relationship was far weaker over the longer period. In other words, imprisonment rates and violent crime rates changed in the same way from 1960 to 1990 (both rose significantly), but not from 1990 to 2019, because in the later period, when crime fell, imprisonment continued to rise.

The combination of a positive relationship between the imprisonment and crime rates in the early part of the sample period and a negative relationship in the latter part yielded a conclusion of no stable relationship between the two variables over the full sample period, and thus an estimated r near zero.

The value of r^2 (actually the square of the r value) indicates the extent to which changes in one variable can be explained by changes in the other variable. Here we see that the variables seemed highly predictive of one another from 1960 to 1990, but that this relationship (or correlation) subsequently vanished (and even reversed) later on.

Prisons weren't the only part of the criminal justice system that grew. All the key components had to be beefed up to prevent bottlenecks in the system. After all, what's the good of additional prisons if there aren't enough police to arrest the criminals, or enough courtrooms and court personnel to try, convict, and sentence them? Given that each state and local government runs its own piece of the system, accomplishing this was quite a challenge.

Under our federal system the federal government has the money but the states and locals have the lion's share of the responsibility for meting out justice. The federal government could expand its own criminal laws, as it did for interstate or cross-border crimes, such as narcotic drug distribution. But too great an expansion raises constitutional red flags.[12] The solution, developed in the late 1960s, was for the federal government to make grants that required the state and local recipients to spend the money as the donor directs, in this case, on strengthening the justice system. The forerunner of this type of legislation was the Omnibus Crime Control and Safe Streets Act of 1968, and many similar statutes followed.[13] The states did their part, adopting myriad laws and policies that beefed up law enforcement. Though it took years, each piece of the system was augmented. The great buildup was underway.

Each part of the justice apparatus had to be built up, starting with the police. Though some departments are better than others at apprehending perpetrators, generally speaking, the more police officers, the more arrests. In 1970 there were 343,669 sworn officers in the United States. By 1990, that had risen 52 percent to 523,262. A decade later, in 2000, the 1970 figure had nearly doubled to 654,601 cops (while the U.S. population rose 38 percent). Did arrests increase? They most certainly did, from 4.9 million in 1970 to 12 million in 2000, a boost of 144 percent. And this doesn't include arrests for minor crimes, the kind that are unlikely to lead to imprisonment.[14]

The next chart shows the strong correlation between the number of police and the number of arrests. The variables rose in tandem during the crime tsunami years, from 1970 to 1995. Then, as crime tailed off, so did arrests, though police numbers continued to grow through 2010. This continued growth reflected fears that the crime decline wouldn't last, plus concern that reducing the number of police prematurely might trigger a crime spike.

The second chart shows how the crime wave correlated with the growth in arrests. It plots the number of violent crimes plus burglary reported to (or witnessed by) the police, along with the number of arrests for those same crimes. Though the number of arrests is much lower than the number of reported crimes—millions of reported crimes are never solved by the police—the two lines on the graph are remarkably interdependent.[15]

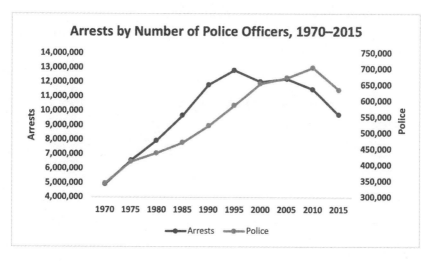

r = 0.9363   r² = 0.8766

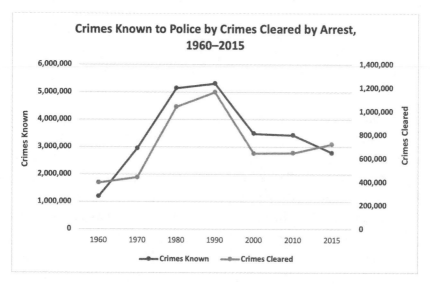

r = 0.9555   r² = 0.9130

Not only do more cops produce more arrests, they also generate more incarcerations. We know this by comparing arrests with admissions to state prisons. Once again, the correlation is striking.

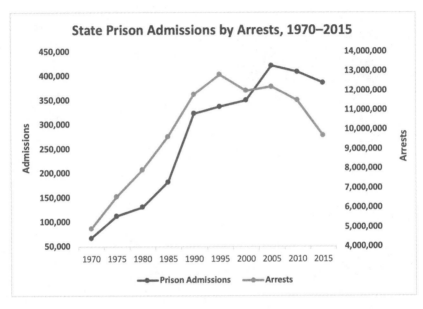

State Prison Admissions by Arrests, 1970–2015

r = 0.8795   r² = 0.7735

Incarceration also requires courtrooms and the personnel who run them: judges, court officers, prosecutors, and defense attorneys. Their numbers grew as well. Assistant prosecutors, the officials who actually handle the cases in big-city criminal courts, increased by 58 percent between 1974 and 2001. And expenditures for taxpayer-funded indigent defense (the overwhelming majority of criminal defendants are too poor to pay for their own attorneys) nearly quadrupled (up 274 percent) between 1979 and 1990. General jurisdiction trial judges (the ones who handle felonies) increased by 88 percent between 1970 and 1998. Other court personnel numbers also swelled: up 261 percent between 1970 and 1990.[16]

Of course, more prisons had to be built too. In 1972–74 there were 631 correctional facilities in the United States, both state and federal institutions. By 1995 that number had mushroomed to 1,306, a 107 percent rise (including 110 privately managed facilities). And even that increase was insufficient. In 2005 the total number of prisons was 1,821.[17]

Jails are one of the few criminal justice components that did not grow. From 1970 to 1993 there actually were 18 percent fewer jails. But not fewer jail inmates. Inmate numbers skyrocketed 186 percent in the same period, as expected given the increase in arrests. Does this suggest overcrowding? Possibly. Or maybe shorter stays. Keep in mind that jails are not prisons. They house most arrestees for a few days and more serious offenders for a few months, until they are transferred to prisons.[18]

The results of the great toughening were positive: crime began to drop in the mid-1990s and it kept dropping. After nearly three decades the tsunami was abating, replaced by a crime trough. Several empirical analyses found a strong relationship between the incarceration buildup and the crime fall. Steven Levitt, of "freakonomics" fame, asserted that the increase in the prison population was the most significant factor in the crime decline of the 1990s. And he wasn't the only one who thought so. An assessment by two other economists of three decades of imprisonment maintained that there was "strong evidence of a negative relationship between prison [population] size and the crime rate." "In a phrase," these authors concluded, "more prison, less crime." Urban policy specialist William Spelman determined that the violent crime decline up to 1997 (really only the start of the crime drop) would have been 27 percent smaller had the prison buildup never occurred.[19]

Of course, what is clear now was not at all certain when the crime turnaround started. During the tsunami years there scarcely was a politician, Democrat or Republican, who failed to address the "law and order" problem, as it came to be known. Even in 1994, which hindsight shows was the start of the big crime drop, Democratic president Bill Clinton proposed a major crime bill and Senator Joe Biden shepherded it through Congress.[20] In the early 1990s, liberal analysts, along with everyone else, had no idea that the great crime decline was around the corner. Consider these words of Professor Lawrence M. Friedman, written in early 1993 to introduce his book on the history of crime and punishment:

> Crime in our decade is a major political issue. Of course, people have always been concerned about crime. But there is reason to believe that people are more upset about crime today than ever before—more worried, more fearful. They are most afraid of sudden violence or theft by strangers; they feel the cities are jungles; they are afraid to walk the streets at night. Millions of parents are afraid their children will turn into junkies. Millions see some sort of rot, some sort of decay infecting society, and crime is the pus oozing out from the wound. . . .
>
> We seem to be in the midst of a horrendous crime storm—a hurricane of crime. The homicide rate in American cities is simply appalling. It takes months or even years for Helsinki or Tokyo to equal the *daily* harvest of rape, pillage, looting, and death in New York City. Why is this happening to us?[21]

9

DENYING THE CRIME TSUNAMI

TO HEAR THE DECARCERATIONISTS TELL IT, the American prison system is an unrelieved horror. A "carceral state," "unprecedented in United States history" (Gottschalk); "a glaring and dreadful stain on the fabric of American history" (Fortner); a "national shame" (Pfaff); a "new Jim Crow" (Alexander); a "vast cruelty" (Bazelon), and on and on. The writers try to outdo each other with memorable condemnations.[1]

The reality of the American justice system is very different. The treatment of prisoners has never been more lenient; boredom is probably their biggest complaint. Compare the brutalities of earlier American punishments described in part 1. Yes, our imprisonment rates are historically high, but they have been retreating for over a decade, and the actual time served—as I'll show in the next chapter—is nowhere near as high as the sentences suggest. Most important, the incarceration buildup did not occur in a vacuum. It was the product of the biggest and most devastating violent crime rise in American history. And the buildup actually reduced crime and saved thousands of lives.

You wouldn't know any of this from reading the endless stream of anti-incarceration books. In fact, most of these tracts deny that there was a crime problem, or ignore it altogether. Despite this glaring short-coming, some of these books have been showered with honors. Michelle Alexander's *The New Jim Crow* was a best seller. Elizabeth Hinton's *From the War on Poverty to the War on Crime* was named one of the one hundred notable books of 2016 by the *New York Times*.[2]

All of these books have one thing in common. They contend that too many people, or too many black people, are behind bars. This assertion is a matter for legitimate debate. Are there, perhaps, too many miscarriages of justice in the American criminal justice system? Or too many minor crimes enforced too aggressively? Are our sentences longer than they need to be to achieve the aims of penology, namely, public protection, offender reform, and retribution (justice) for wrongdoing? Has the system become too costly for the benefits provided? Does it discriminate on grounds of race, treating blacks and whites differently despite comparable circumstances?

These contentions, and others that readers can no doubt think of, are certainly fair grounds for discussion. But that conversation must be based on realities. To paraphrase Daniel Patrick Moynihan, everyone is entitled to his own opinion, but not his own facts. Too often, however, the mass incarceration books, in their zeal for decarceration, make a deeply disturbing claim. This is the astonishing argument that there was no crime rise beginning in the late 1960s, or that the increase in imprisonment had nothing to do with crime, and that it was, instead, a product of other causes. Even the so-called gold standard for research on criminal justice, the National Academy of Sciences, presents a highly misleading description of the biggest crime boom in American history. "Over the four decades when incarceration rates steadily rose, U.S. crime rates showed no clear trend: the rate of violent crime rose, then fell, rose again, then declined sharply."[3] No clear trend? The two-

and-a-half-decade rise in crime was relentless and alarming except for a brief minor downturn in the early 1980s that proved to be a false alarm. Actually, from the mid-1970s to the mid-1990s, both crime and incarceration rates escalated in tandem, only diverging distinctly at the start of the twenty-first century.

Sometimes there is no discussion of crime at all in these books, so that the millions of murdered, maimed, and traumatized crime victims—many of whom were African Americans—are rendered invisible. This reminds me of the old joke in which the bloody and bruised boxer begs his corner man to throw in the towel. The corner man, not wanting his guy to lose heart, assures the fighter that his opponent barely laid a glove on him. "Yeah?" says the hapless warrior. "Then you better watch the referee, cause someone is beating the hell outta me." Sorry, but the criminal justice referee was not responsible for the mass mugging of America.

We need to set the historical record straight. It is not only important that we get the history right for accuracy's sake. We had better ground our contemporary policy decisions in reality if we want them to be effective and economical. Consider the oft-expressed claim that drug prosecutions are responsible for the high rates of imprisonment of African Americans. This is, as I will show, absolutely false. So, if we revise our drug laws to fix this non-problem, we might get more drug trafficking, but we will not significantly reduce black incarceration.

It is time to take a hard look at some of the decarceration literature, to separate truth from fiction and face the realities of crime and punishment.

* * *

Let us begin with the book that seems to have launched the industry, Michelle Alexander's highly acclaimed *The New Jim Crow*.[4] One would be hard-pressed to find in this work any discussion of crime. On the face of it a reader might consider it quite astonishing that any serious discussion of incarceration could completely ignore crime, as if crime and punishment were unrelated. As noted previously, there is a weak defense for this position based on the imperfect correlation between the volume of crime and the response of the criminal justice system. There is, however, a good explanation for the anomaly. Usually there is a time lag between the rise or fall in crime and the response of the criminal justice system. It takes time to change a system run by fifty independent states. And it takes time to build or downsize the criminal justice infrastructure (cops, courts, and corrections facilities) needed to effect the change. But a lag is one thing; suggesting that crime levels and punishment policies are altogether unrelated is quite another. This is one of those fictions that underpins the decarceration movement.

Alexander adopts an inflated, and essentially dishonest, definition of mass incarceration. She then presents a patently false explanation for the growth in imprisonment, attributing it to drug prosecutions, when in fact crimes of violence were much more significant. First, the definitional problem.

Alexander equates mass incarceration with "correctional control," even though the overwhelming majority of people under such "control" are at large in the community. "The most important fact to keep in mind," she tells us, is that "debates about prison statistics ignore the fact that most people who are under correctional control today are not in prison." They are, she points out, "on probation or parole, primarily for nonviolent offenses."[5] In fact, only one-third of criminal defendants in the United States are incarcerated in prison or jail; two-thirds are free on probation or parole.[6]

But there is a big difference between freedom, even qualified freedom, and being locked up. Is there any defendant who would prefer a prison sentence to probation? Is there a prisoner who wouldn't trade his cell for parole? Release is the opposite of incarceration, and community corrections is considered by most a Progressive alternative. Probation gives defendants who have been adjudicated guilty a chance to avoid prison, saves society the expense of confining them, helps maintain families intact, and, if applied to the appropriate defendant, improves the likelihood of rehabilitation. If anything, the decarceration push spearheaded by Alexander and others may result in an increase in the proportion of offenders in the community as an alternative to imprisonment.[7]

Incarceration, mass or otherwise, should not be inflated to include its very opposite, non-incarceration. This is especially true when the non-incarcerative controls imposed by the criminal justice system are minimal.

Roughly 3.5 million people in the United States are on probation. That is a big number, but probationers are not only unconfined; they are virtually unrestricted. When convicted, a probationer usually will be admonished by the judge to refrain from carrying a gun or doing drugs, to seek employment and to periodically report to a probation officer. The main restriction is to desist from any additional crimes. It is not hard to meet these requirements. Millions comply. Probation terms usually run from one to three years, at the end of which, if the probationer has met the few demands placed on him, he will no longer be under so-called correctional control.

In recent years, more than six out of ten probationers have been convicted of felonies, 22 percent have committed violent crimes, and 26 percent drug offenses.[8] Alexander is correct to say that probationers' offenses are, in the main, nonviolent. That is one big reason why they are released. But her implication that drug crimes are responsible for the millions on probation is obviously incorrect since three-quarters of all probationers were *not* sentenced for drug offenses.

So, drugs are not driving the probation figures. Nor is race. Since 2000, fewer than one-third of all probationers have been black.[9] This is out of proportion to the black general population, which was about 12 percent of the nation, but not out of proportion to black offending.[10] Even Alexander concedes (though it's buried in her book) that there is a black crime problem. "Black men do have much higher rates of violent crime" than whites, she acknowledges, and "violent crime is concentrated in ghetto communities."[11]

Parole, which Alexander lumps with probation, is a considerably different matter. True, parole is also a release into the general population, but it is a release for those who have been convicted of serious crimes and have served a part of their sentence in prison. This is a more dangerous population than probationers. Eighty-three percent of parolees are arrested for additional crimes within nine years of their release, and 39 percent of these arrests are for violent crimes.[12] Parolees, like probationers, are also under restrictions—no associating with criminals, no drugs or excessive alcohol, no guns, and, of course, no more crime. Still, the parolee is free, and should not be counted as part of the incarcerated population.

A disproportionate number of parolees—30 to 40 percent in the last two decades—have been African American.[13] But why is this so? The answer is clear. Given high levels of black offending, high rates of imprisonment follow, and early release from prison, that is, parole, is the inevitable next step. So, we need to look closely at imprisonment, especially of African Americans. What we will see is that violent crimes and not drug offenses were accountable, and still are responsible, for black imprisonment.

Alexander denies this. She states in no uncertain terms, "Violent crime is *not* responsible for mass incarceration."[14] So let us examine this claim with some unimpeachable statistics. Suppose we could end the War on Drugs and remove all drug inmates, regardless of race, from state prisons. Would this dramatically reduce the black prison population, as Alexander implies? According to the most recent report of the U.S. Justice Department's Bureau of Justice Statistics, there are in state prisons 409,600 black inmates, 394,800 non-Hispanic whites, and 274,300 Hispanics, for a total population of 1,078,700.[15] Blacks, therefore, constitute 37.97 percent of the state prison population. Among these inmates, the following were sentenced for drug offenses: 52,100 blacks, 64,500 whites, and 28,800 Hispanics. (Note that many more whites than blacks are serving time for drug crimes.) Removing all the drug inmates would reduce the black prisoner count to 357,500, the white to 330,300, and the Hispanic to 245,500, for a total of 933,300. After the removal of the drug offenders, blacks would make up 38.30 percent of the inmate population, an *increase* of .33 percentage points over the actual distribution. In other words, eliminating drug convictions and sentences wouldn't reduce the proportion of prisoners who are African Americans, it would leave it essentially unchanged.

Clearly, ending the War on Drugs would have a negligible impact on the percentage of state prisoners who are African American. Drug crimes explain only 13 percent of black state imprisonments, whereas violent crimes account for 62 percent.[16] Federal prisons are a different story. Since they house only federal law violators, they hold few inmates (of any race) guilty of ordinary street crimes, such as common burglaries, robberies, and assaults. Those offenses are outside federal jurisdiction. But drugs commonly cross state or national boundaries, so drug crimes are federal (as well as state) offenses. Consequently, drug traffickers (with a sprinkling of drug possessors), make up a sizable proportion (46 percent) of federal prisoners. But this doesn't significantly affect the total U.S. prison population since federal inmates are only 11 percent of all prisoners.[17] If we combine all black drug offenders, state and federal, drug sentences account for only 5.5 percent of the African Americans in prison. In other words, contrary to Alexander, more than *ninety-four out of one hundred African American prisoners, state and federal, are serving time for non-drug offenses.*

Even more damning: drug crimes have been responsible for only one-quarter of black state imprisonments for at least the last twenty-five years. That is why analysts like law professor John Pfaff called Alexander's claim that drug crimes were responsible for the growth in imprisonment, that is, for so-called mass incarceration, "blatantly false."[18] Consider the situation during the height of the crack cocaine era, which ran from the late 1980s to the early 1990s. Imprisonment rates in the United States had been rising since the mid-1970s, but drugs were not nearly the problem they would become in the crack years. In 1980, for instance, when cocaine was a relatively minor menace, only 6 percent of state prisoners were in for drug crimes. By 1990, when the War on Drugs was in high gear, this figure jumped to 22 percent. Unquestionably a big increase, but note that even at the height of the drug war, 78 percent of all state prisoners were behind bars for non-drug crimes.[19]

And what impact on African Americans? In 1991, the first year with prison statistics broken out by race and crime, 25 percent of black state prisoners were sentenced for drug offenses. Even at the apogee of crack prosecutions, three-quarters of all black state inmates were imprisoned for something other than drug crimes.[20] This percentage held steady throughout the 1990s, and then started declining until the present 13 percent rate.[21]

Why, then, were more blacks than ever imprisoned in the 1990s? The answer is violent crime, not drugs. Half the growth in black state prisoners from 1990 to 1999 was due to violent crime, 27 percent to drug offenses. During this same period, 46–48 percent of all black inmates in state prisons had been sentenced for a crime of violence.[22]

The conclusion is clear: violent crime, not the drug war, was the main reason so many African Americans were behind bars—and that is still true today. Michelle Alexander is simply wrong.

* * *

One of the decarcerationists' favorite counterarguments is the claim that African American crime rates are not really that high, they're merely a by-product of police bias. The contention is that police, due to implicit race bias, arrest blacks more than whites despite similar misconduct. Consequently, this line of reasoning continues, more African Americans are incarcerated even though whites commit a comparable number of crimes on a per capita basis.

Numerous empirical studies have purported to find such police bias. However, according to two Harvard sociologists, many if not most of these studies are flawed because they don't take account of common police practices, such as deployments to high-crime areas or locations with more serious crimes. Instead, they make indefensible assumptions that police treat all areas of a city the same.[23]

In fact, deploying police in greater numbers to communities of color probably has nothing to do with bias. Rather, deployments are a race-neutral response to the high levels of crime in (and 911 calls from) those locales. As a matter of fact, African Americans have long pressed for more police protection from violent criminals and drug dealers.[24]

Nor need we rely on police-generated data alone as proof of high black crime rates. There is evidence independent of the criminal justice system—from crime victim surveys and from homicide mortality records—that refutes the bias claim. Crime victim surveys provide powerful proof that arrests are not tainted by race bias. Keep in mind that the survey respondents—crime victims—are ordinary citizens without any incentive to misidentify the race of their assailants.

Every year since 1973 the Census Bureau has been conducting the National Crime Victimization Survey (NCVS), a huge study of criminal victimization. The latest poll involved interviews with 249,000 people. This is massive as surveys go, and therefore very reliable. In 2018 the victims of violent incidents reported that 29 percent of the perpetrators were African Americans.[25] This is more than twice the percentage of blacks in the United States, currently 12.5 percent. (Fifty-two percent of the assailants were identified as whites, considerably *less* than the white proportion of the population, which is 60 percent.) In short, African Americans were substantially overrepresented among violent incident perpetrators.

Many of the violent incidents described to the poll takers were never reported to the police, but of those that were, 35 percent involved alleged black perpetrators. When the police made arrests in these incidents, 33 percent of the arrestees were persons of color. In other words, police arrested *fewer* blacks percentage-wise than were reported to them. This shows a lack of race bias in arrests. Had the police been biased, we would expect the percentage of arrests of African Americans to have been *greater* than 35 percent.

When it comes to serious crimes—the ones that send people to prison—arrests are not discretionary, so there is little room for discrimination. Most of the studies purporting to find bias involve minor offenses, such as marijuana possession, or relatively minor intrusions, such as street stops and frisks. These are discretionary acts: police don't have to stop and frisk a particular individual, and they may issue a warning instead of arresting a low-level offender. So here is where the bias—if there is any—comes into play. But arrests for serious crimes, such as murder, rape, robbery, aggravated assault, felony theft, and burglary, are not discretionary. When the police learn of such crimes, they have to arrest the suspects should they find them. And these are the arrests that send people to prison and therefore produce so-called mass incarceration. Arrests for serious crimes are much less susceptible to police bias, especially since these arrestees will be carefully vetted by prosecutors, defense attorneys, judges, and (sometimes) juries.

The bottom line is that high rates of violent crime among African Americans are not a function of police bias. They are, uncomfortable as it may make us, a social reality. Even Michelle Alexander admits it, if grudgingly.

* * *

A more recent entry in the anti-incarceration sweepstakes is Elizabeth Hinton's *From the War on Poverty to the War on Crime.*[26] This tendentious history purports to trace the origins of our various domestic "military" campaigns against social problems. According to Hinton, the War on Crime and its offshoot War on Drugs originated with President Lyndon Johnson's war on poverty of the late 1960s. Antipoverty and law enforcement programs were fused under Johnson as part of a liberal effort to "improve American society." In the 1970s, under President Richard Nixon, the anticrime policies became independent and allegedly malign. These policies, Hinton asserts, "were built on a set of racist assumptions" developed out of the work of Daniel Patrick Moynihan, Edward C. Banfield, and James Q. Wilson. "All three came to see black poverty as a fact of American life and crime and violence as somehow innate among African Americans." As a result, the War on Crime took a punitive turn, aimed at young black males. "Marred by racism," Hinton charges, "the deliberate arrest and incarceration of young African

American men became a strategy to prevent future crime."[27]

Note well this last accusation: the Nixon administration intentionally locked up black men, not because they were criminals, but because they were black and ostensibly criminogenic, that is, crime-prone. Such an urban removal policy is redolent of the Black Codes of the nineteenth-century South, or the internment of Japanese Americans during World War II. Even Michelle Alexander wasn't brazen enough to level such a charge. But Hinton does not provide much proof for her outrageous claim.

I first consider Hinton's assertion that Moynihan, Banfield, and James Q. Wilson "helped push the Nixon administration toward an understanding of black cultural pathology, rather than poverty, as the root cause of crime."[28] Obviously, she doesn't understand their views, which were different from one another, and can only be characterized as "racist" by reducing that term to an epithet devoid of serious content.

Edward Banfield, for instance, expressly denied that there was much significance to African American culture as an explanation for crime. He believed that the key to explaining high black crime rates and other antisocial behaviors, such as rioting, was social class. "It is very unlikely," he wrote in his attention-grabbing work, *The Unheavenly City*, "that any differences in racial (or ethnic) culture will have as much explanatory importance . . . as do differences in income, education and class culture."[29] While, according to Banfield, poverty per se is not the key determinant of crime, the attitudes associated with low income and education are. There is nothing racist in this thinking, as it does not assert that race is a determinant of behavior. Nor is there any contention or implication that crime and violence are "somehow innate" among African Americans. To the contrary, Banfield believed that African American crime rates will decline when blacks, like the nineteenth-century Irish, move into the middle-class—a movement he thought "inexorable."[30]

James Q. Wilson's writings of the 1970s scarcely discuss African Americans and crime. In his best-known book on criminality, aptly titled *Thinking about Crime*, first published in 1975, there is no talk of a black social pathology and little discussion of blacks at all.[31] Wilson does examine problematic relations between blacks and police—a discussion worth reexamination today—but that is the only extended discussion of African Americans in the book.[32]

Wilson's prescriptions for the criminal justice system are modest and do not allude to race or African Americans. For instance, he would encourage "self-help organizations of citizens" in neighborhoods "threatened with crime or disorder." These organizations, "working in collaboration with the police," would patrol their communities to "detect, though not to apprehend, suspicious persons."[33] Presumably, this proposal would include black communities, though Wilson does not mention African Americans in this section. In fact, black Muslims did patrol housing projects in African Americans neighborhoods. And there has been, since the George Floyd protests of 2020, renewed talk of community-based policing. Certainly, Wilson's self-help proposal is a far cry from any plan to arrest and incarcerate blacks.

With regard to incarceration, Wilson recommends that "persons convicted of committing minor offenses who have little or no prior record . . . be dealt with by community-based corrections," that is, kept out of jail or prison. The most serious punishments, he urges, should be imposed in accordance with sentencing guidelines on high-rate, that is, repeat, offenders, with release determined by the sentencing judge, not correctional authorities. Shorter sentences should be given to low-rate defendants. Anything "racist" in these proposals would be difficult to find.[34]

Almost a decade later, in his famous "broken windows" essay, Wilson urged police to clamp down on low-level offenses as a remedy for urban disorder and a way of staving off community decline into serious crime.[35] It is possible, perhaps probable, that low-level arrests had a bigger impact on blacks than whites because of the high proportion of African Americans residing in central cities. But if so, it was because of black overinvolvement in low-level urban offenses—actual involvement, not some anticipatory preventative. In any event, arrests for low-level offenses do not lead to significant periods of incarceration. Unless the arrested person is also wanted for more serious crimes, arrests for minor offenses usually result in a few days or at most, a few weeks in jail, and no time in prison. Broken Windows policy was not designed to, and did not in actuality, incapacitate blacks as a way of heading off crime.

In the 1970s, when Wilson was advising Nixon, nothing in his writings in any way supported a "black social pathology" explanation for crime. Nor do his subsequent works, written in the 1980s, though the later writings are not relevant to his views in the earlier decade, which are the focal point of Hinton's analysis.[36]

Daniel Patrick Moynihan's 1965 report on the Negro family comes the closest to supporting Hinton's contention that Nixon's advisors saw black cultural pathology, not poverty, as the root cause of crime.[37] Moynihan, employed by President Johnson's Department of Labor at the time, actually used the phrase "tangle of pathology" in his report. He probably got it from the influential African American psychologist Kenneth B. Clark, who wrote of the black ghetto's "tangle of community and personal pathology."[38] For Moynihan, a tangle of pathologies meant various interrelated African American social problems—crime, delinquency, addiction, and welfare dependancy—that he traced to the decline of the two-parent black family. "Most Negro youth," he wrote,

> are in *danger* of being caught up in the tangle of pathology that affects their world. . . . [A]t the center of the tangle of pathology is the weakness of the family structure. Once or twice removed, it will be found to be the principal source of most of the aberrant, inadequate, or anti-social behavior that . . . serves to perpetuate the cycle of poverty and deprivation.[39]

Moynihan's discussion of African American crime and delinquency focused on the effect of fatherless homes. There isn't a hint of a suggestion, however, that black incarceration was a solution. Rather, he proposed "a national effort . . . directed towards the question of family structure" with the objective of "strengthen[ing] the Negro family."[40]

Hinton declares cultural pathology theories like Moynihan's to be "racist," but she offers no justification or explanation for the label.[41] It is little more than an epithet, applied to views with which the name-caller disagrees. To be consistent, it should also apply to Kenneth Clark, the highly respected black scholar, who called the dark ghetto "institutionalized pathology."[42] It was Clark who wrote the following, though Moynihan could just as well have been the author.

> Not only is the pathology of the ghetto self-perpetuating, but one kind of pathology breeds another. The child born in the ghetto is more likely to come into a world of broken homes and illegitimacy; and this family and social instability is conducive to delinquency, drug addiction, and criminal violence.[43]

The Moynihan Report was written in the mid-1960s, well before its author went to work for Nixon. In early 1970, one year after Nixon took office, Moynihan drafted the highly publicized "benign neglect" memo to the president, widely interpreted by the Left as advocating indifference to black problems.[44] Hinton's spin is that Moynihan had become fatalistic about black social progress: "his call for "benign neglect" implied that the "tangle of pathology" could not be broken after all."[45]

In truth, the memo was the very opposite of indifferent, but it advised the president to tone down the racial rhetoric because the subject "has been too much talked about." More to the point, Moynihan told Nixon that "apart from white racial attitudes . . . anti-social behavior among young black males is the biggest problem black Americans face." Moynihan did not make any policy recommendations regarding crime, however, because he felt that they needed to "be getting on with research . . . We just don't know enough," he concluded.[46]

Soon afterwards, Moynihan became part of an inner-circle crime policy team that ultimately made recommendations to Nixon, leading to the replacement of the war on poverty metaphor with the wars on crime and drugs. Nixon then signed seven executive orders related to crime and three major pieces of legislation, but none of them supported preventative incapacitation of African Americans.[47] In fact, they sometimes made the law more lenient. The 1970 Controlled Substances Act, for example, abolished nearly all mandatory minimum sentences for federal drug offenses.[48] By 1973, Moynihan was appointed ambassador to India, and went on to serve as United Nations delegate under President Gerald Ford. He consequently changed focus from domestic to foreign affairs.

In summary, Hinton correctly identifies Moynihan as endorsing a theory of black cultural deficiency, but she presents no evidence that he supported a policy of preemptive incapacitation of blacks. Nor does she explain why she believes Moynihan's views are "racist." There isn't a shred of evidence to prove that Moynihan, Wilson, or Banfield endorsed any policy to incarcerate African Americans in order to prevent crime. They undoubtedly did recommend a beefing up of the criminal justice system— the War on Crime—but such a policy shift was essential since crime, riots, bombings, and disorder were rampant in the United States of the 1970s.

Even if Hinton's outrageous claim were true, it would have been impossible to implement such a scheme in post–civil rights America. Hinton doesn't seem to appreciate that each decision to incarcerate someone for a crime must be approved by a court, and American judges would never have facilitated such a shocking and grossly unconstitutional policy. Nor would Congress, the media, or even the general public (frightened though they were) have countenanced it. After all, less than a decade earlier, the nation supported the most sweeping civil rights legislation in over a century. Moreover, especially after the Voting Rights Act of 1965, blacks acquired enough political clout to have effectively vetoed any such scheme. Indeed, elements of the black community pushed for more law enforcement, not less, as crime increasingly ravaged their communities.[49]

One wouldn't know this from Hinton's book, which scarcely discusses these issues. Instead, she ties the fictitious black removal policy to allegedly flawed criminal justice data.

The calculated decision to remove low-income youth of color from their neighborhoods was justified and reinforced by new data on African American crime that appeared in the early 1970s—data that were the product of the modernization of police departments and the new state criminal justice bureaucracies established during the prior decade.[50]

One might have thought that improved data collection processes were a good thing, as they produce more accurate and complete information. But since they pointed to excessive African American offending rates (and, of course, victimization rates, which Hinton conveniently omits), she supposes they must have been faulty. "Throughout the 1960s and 1970s," Hinton says, "flawed statistical data overstated the problem of crime in African American communities and produced a distorted picture of American crime as a whole."[51] And what evidence does she have for this claim? She makes four points.

First, she says, the "FBI's Uniform Crime Report [UCR] failed to measure beyond the point of arrest, and thus did not account for whether or not suspects were ever eventually convicted."[52] It is, of course, correct to say that the UCR, which presents only police-generated data, does not cover convictions. But even the beginning student of criminal justice knows that reports of crime, such as 911 calls to the police, are a much better indicator of the realities of criminal activity than convictions. The most common criticism of the UCR is that it *undercounts* crime due to the failure of victims to report incidents to the police.[53] Relying on convictions would only worsen the inaccuracy, as a mere fraction of actual criminal incidents result in conviction. To the extent that the FBI's *Uniform Crime Reports* are flawed, it is in the direction of underestimating the occurrence of crime.

Her second argument is that while "African Americans had the highest rate of arrest for crimes of murder, robbery, and rape, . . . these crimes also had the lowest percentage of arrestees who eventually faced prosecution and trial."[54] If Hinton is referring to the percentage of reported crimes solved by the police, her assertion is plainly false with respect to murder, which has long had the highest percentage of police clearances of any crime.[55] As for robbery and rape, though police clearance rates are lower than the rates for murder (roughly half in the case of robbery), this has no bearing on the proportion of arrestees who are black. If, on the other hand, Hinton is implying that black arrests are less likely to hold up in court (i.e., black arrestees are more likely than white defendants to be released without formal charges), she needs to provide evidence of this. Unsurprisingly, she offers none.

Third, Hinton discounts the elevated African American arrest rates as artifacts of the high numbers of police assigned to black communities. This argument has already been explored. I would simply add here that arrest rates of blacks (and whites) increased as crime rose from the 1970s to the 1990s, and Hinton would have to show that the mounting arrests of African Americans were more a function of increased deployments than higher crime.[56] This, too, she fails to do. Furthermore, since police are required to respond to civilian reports of crime incidents, if they get more calls from black neighborhoods, they will assign more police to those locations. Moreover, given the elevated black-on-black crime rates, calls to the police by black crime victims or witnesses are likely to result in the arrest of an African American suspect. When it comes to serious crimes and nondiscretionary arrests, police deployments are not the driver. Rather, both arrests and deployments are driven by high African American crime victimization rates.

Finally, Hinton says that FBI data "emphasized street crime to the exclusion of organized and white-collar crime," skewing the data and the resulting policies toward "the crimes committed by low-income and unemployed Americans."[57] As a matter of simple logic, however, the lack of white-collar offenses in FBI reports does not invalidate the data on rising street crime or black involvement in it. (Local police are not usually involved with white-collar crime, which is left to federal agents or investigative bodies, so they don't collect data on such offenses or report them to the FBI.) Moreover, it is street crimes that terrified the public, and especially the African American public, which was disproportionally victimized by such offenses. That alone is reason enough for separate statistics for predatory crimes, just as the UCR provides. In any event, African Americans have high rates of white-collar crime too.[58]

Contrary to Hinton, street crime was real and it was surging. UCR data indicate that white involvement in crime rose nearly as dramatically as black. Arrest rates of whites for violent crime in 1990 were 3.4 times the 1965 rates.[59] Moreover, there are multiple sources of crime data, all of which indicate that crime was rising from the 1970s on, and rising substantially. Hinton's efforts to discredit the UCR—totally unpersuasive though they are—still leave these other indicators intact. For instance, the National Crime Victims' Survey (NCVS) showed, like the UCR, increasing violence until the early 1980s, followed by a brief downturn, and then another surge from the late 1980s to the early 1990s, fueled by the crack cocaine epidemic that overwhelmed communities of color.

The accompanying chart, derived from crime victim surveys, shows violent victimization rates from 1973 on, when the NCVS began, a time when violent crime was already elevated. Rates climbed 10 percent by 1981, retreated by 20 percent for the next four years, only to escalate in excess of 16 percent from 1987 to 1994. Then followed the great crime decline, from 1995 on. None of these figures are derived from police reports.

Source: U.S. Department of Justice, Bureau of Justice Statistics, *Key Facts at a Glance, National Crime Victimization Survey Violent Crime Trends, 1973–2001.*

Likewise, homicide mortality data, which reflect deaths caused by human agency whether or not they lead to criminal charges, also confirm the upswing in violence. These figures, produced from county medical examiner reports throughout the United States, are collected and published by the federal Centers for Disease Control and Prevention (CDC). They too are developed autonomously, and there is no reason to believe they are anything but accurate. The huge increase in homicide rates from the 1970s to the 1990s is obvious and consistent with the UCR data.

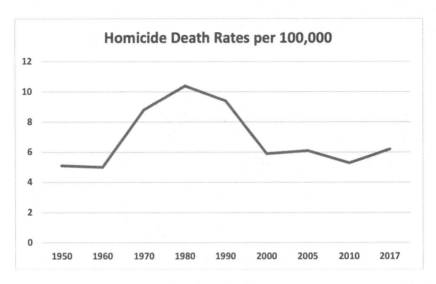

Source: Centers for Disease Control and Prevention, *Health, United States, 2018*, table 5, https://www.cdc.gov/nchs/data/hus/2018/005.pdf.

When multiple measures of crime, compiled independently, point in the same direction and also confirm the common experience of those who lived through the period, one needs to come to terms with reality.

Ironically, Hinton completely contradicts her own arguments by admitting that crime "drastically increased both in statistical measures and as a reality in low-income urban neighborhoods."[60] She says this to prove that the War on Crime failed—another questionable assertion. Obviously, she wants to have it both ways: the amount of crime was "overstated," and yet it "drastically increased." She was right the second time.

10

THE MYTH OF OVERPUNISHMENT

BY HISTORICAL MEASURES the American system of criminal justice has become radically less punitive. In the last fifty years, corporal punishment, the death penalty, and overt racism have become rarities. Prisoners today are permitted family and conjugal visitations; they have libraries, gyms, television, email, and internet access; they get free lawyers to handle their appeals as well as advanced medical care in case of health problems—all at public expense.

Despite the unprecedented leniency, critics of the system—the decarcerationists—persist in claiming that we overpunish. They point to high incarceration rates even though imprisonment rates are at a twenty-five-year low and black imprisonment rates tumbled 29 percent in the last decade.[1] They decry long sentences without examining the actual time served. They compare the United States to other countries while ignoring major differences between us and them. Some call for arbitrary reductions in our prison and jail populations, such as 39 or even 50 percent, without regard to crime rates.[2] Others push for the total abolition of prisons despite the lack of any workable alternative.[3]

No one disputes that our imprisonment rates—the number of prisoners per capita—are historically high. The United States had over 1.4 million prisoners at year-end 2019, for a rate of 419 per 100,000. But the justice system buildup that led to these rates was a direct response to the massive crime wave of the 1960s-1990s. Moreover, imprisonment rates are steadily declining; the 2019 rate is the lowest in 24 years, dating back to 1995.[4]

In absolute terms, the prison population is a tiny fraction of the adult population of the country. All state and federal prisoners combined total only 0.6 percent of the 18-and-over population of the United States. If we add in parolees, those released from prison after serving a portion of their terms, the total comes to a mere 0.9 percent. In positive terms, 99.1 percent of Americans are not serving time (or were not recently released) for the most dangerous and disturbing crimes. Furthermore, those who are imprisoned are overwhelmingly recidivists; five out of six are arrested again once they are released. The same cohort reoffends repeatedly until taken out of action by the justice system.[45] About 5 percent of the United States population—the "ravenous wolves"—is responsible for 47-55 percent of all crime.[56]

Imprisonment rates are only part of the picture. They say nothing about the reasons for our high incarceration levels. We can't tell if we over-incarcerate without looking at crime and punishment in greater detail.

If our rates are excessive, it must be due to one of two causes, or some mix of both. Either we are locking up too many people or we are keeping them behind bars too long. Neither of these claims holds up to close scrutiny.

It will be difficult to claim that too many people are incarcerated when we examine the number of unpunished crimes. We know from the federal government's massive National Crime Victimization Survey (249,000 interviewees in 2019) that a high percentage of serious crimes are never reported to the police or are never solved if they are reported. Consider just four crimes of violence, the kind of offenses that surely deserve imprisonment: murder, rape, robbery and aggravated assault. Note the attrition as we move from the number of each crime reported in the victims' survey to the number known to police, and on to arrests and imprisonment. While nearly half of murderers were caught and imprisoned, less than 6 percent of the other violent offenders met a similar fate. Though these figures are just for one year (2019), they recur with comparable attrition rates annually.

CRIMES RESULTING IN IMPRISONMENT, 2019[67]

Crime	Claimed by Victims	Known to Police	Arrests	Admitted to Prison
Murder	--	16,425	9,352	8,033 [48.9%]
Rape	459,310	139,815	19,592	22,583 [4.9%]
Robbery	534,420	267,988	65,560	30,385 [5.7%]
Agg. Assault	1,019,490	821,182	317,632	55,268 [5.4%]

Notes: Murder includes non-negligent manslaughter. Prison admissions for rape include other sexual offenses. Prison admissions for assault include aggravated and simple assault. Prison admissions in 2019 include some crimes committed and arrests made in previous years.

Moving on to the reasons for imprisonment, it becomes even more apparent that we aren't incarcerating too many people. First, a majority of inmates in state prisons—56 percent—are serving time for extremely violent crimes, including murder, rape, robbery, or assault. No one can seriously argue that such crimes should be punished lightly. The following table shows the percentage of inmates sentenced for each type of crime. (The table covers state prisons only, which house 88 percent of the U.S. prison population.)

Type of Crime	% of Prisoners	Offenses Included
Violent	55.5%	Murder, rape, robbery, assault, sexual assault, and other crimes of violence
Property	16%	Burglary, theft, motor vehicle theft, fraud, and other property crimes
Drug	14.1%	Possession (3.7%), trafficking and other (10.4%)
Public Order	12.3%	Weapons offenses, driving while intoxicated, and other public order offenses

The remaining crimes by inmates may not be violent per se, but they are frequently associated with risks to public safety, such as with drug trafficking, weapons crimes, and drunk driving. Sixteen percent of the nonviolent sentences are for serious property crimes, including burglary and felony theft. Fourteen percent are for drug crimes, only a small proportion of which (3.7 percent) are for mere possession rather than the more serious trafficking. The rest of the inmate population, 12 percent, is serving time for so-called public order crimes, including illegal gun possession, which certainly involves the risk of violence.[7]

Not only are the inmates' crimes serious, but they usually have long records of other grave offenses. A sample of 404,638 state prisoners released in 2005 found that they had been arrested before their imprisonment a jaw-dropping total of 4.3 million times, which comes to almost eleven arrests per prisoner. A follow-up study found that after release, 83 percent of these same prisoners were rearrested within nine years of discharge.[8] Most people would agree that incorrigibility is an appropriate factor in deciding whether or not a convicted individual belongs in prison. High-rate offenders also get longer sentences, which, as I'll explain momentarily, raises incarceration rates.

Given the nature of their offenses, along with their lengthy records of lawlessness, there is little basis for claims of overpunishment. Prison inmates have done terrible crimes, and they break the law repeatedly. They have little regard for the law or their fellow human beings. The public knows this even if the decarcerationists do not (or won't admit it if they do). Of course, there are and always will be "*60 Minutes*" cases: isolated miscarriages of justice. These cases are deeply disturbing. But they are the inevitable by-products of fallible human judgment, and outliers seldom provide guidance for reordering our criminal justice system. Hard cases, as the lawyers say, make bad law.

There always will be tension between the need to protect the innocent and the obligation to punish the guilty, but the current American system does a tolerable job of both. The fact is, the overwhelming majority of prison inmates are guilty of serious crimes that pose significant risks to the American public. Any argument for a dramatic downscaling of our sentencing policies will have to address these realities of imprisonment.

* * *

The second contention of the incarceration critics is that we are imposing too much punishment on prisoners. To stake out this claim, they cite the lengthy sentences imposed. Historian Marie Gottschalk, for instance, complains that the United States "remains deeply attached to condemning huge numbers of offenders to extremely long sentences," apparently unaware that few inmates actually serve such stretches.[9] Sentences are misleading since between parole and "good time" release only around 20 percent of inmates serve full terms.[10] In addition, many convicted defendants are given no-incarceration sentences to begin with. In fact, 31 percent of all convicted felons and 23 percent of violent offenders are released without spending a single day in prison.[11]

For those offenders who are imprisoned, the time actually served, not sentences, should be used to properly gauge the extent of their punishment. It may surprise you to learn that on average, released prisoners serve only 2.6 years and the median time served is a mere one year and four months.[12]

TIME ACTUALLY SERVED BY STATE PRISONERS RELEASED IN 2016[13]

Offense	Median	Mean
Murder	13.4 years	15 years
Rape/sexual assault	4.2 years	6.2 years
Robbery	3.2 years	4.7 years
Burglary	1.4 years	2.2 years
Assault	1.4 years	2.5 years
Drugs	1.2 years	1.8 years

As one would expect, murderers serve far and away the most time, followed by rapists. In the last twenty years, these two crimes have seen significant increases in prison time. But punishments for the other offenses in the table have not risen greatly over the last seven decades. Take robbery and assault, for example, two crimes of violence. Before 1970, which is to say, before the great crime tsunami, robbers served a median three years for their crimes, while those committing felonious assault did less than two years.[14] In 2016 robbers served a bit over three years while assault earned the offender less than a year and a half. The 2016 punishments were virtually the same as the penalties received in the 1950s and 1960s—a tad higher for robbery and somewhat lower for assault.

The graph provides the trend in time served for seven crimes.[15] These punishments started to rise significantly in the 1990s, just as the crime wave was starting to wind down. For incarceration critics this was the big "aha"; why, they ask, should punishments increase when crime is going down? There are two good answers. First, no one knew that crime was on its way south. It had declined before, in the early 1980s, only to rise again by the end of the decade. That's why all the politicians at the time—the Clintons and Joe Biden included—supported the 1994 crime bill. Second, there is compelling reason to believe that the incarceration buildup helped bring about the decline, so why would anyone play with fire and reverse course?

After 2008 the time served for rape dropped precipitously and imprisonment for robbery, assault, burglary, and drugs sank back to pre–crime tsunami levels or even lower. In retrospect, it is clear that the mid-1990s to early 2000s were a lag period, a time when punishments had not yet caught up with declining crime.

In sum, except for murder and manslaughter, actual time behind bars is in line with historical practice in the United States. And with the decline in the use of the death penalty, the punishment for murderers has become more, not less, lenient.

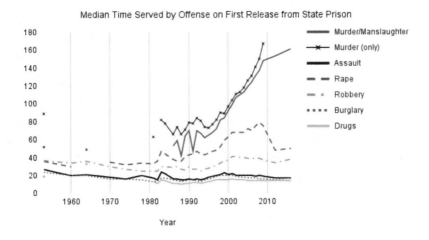

Median Time Served by Offense on First Release from State Prison

Decarcerationists also frequently compare the United States to Europe, where the imprisonment rates are much lower. Our rates, 432 per 100,000 in 2018, are more than four times Europe's and in excess of three times that of neighboring Canada.[16] But imprisonment rates alone are not the best measure of punitiveness because they do not tell us enough about the volume of crime. Imagine two countries, one with an exceptionally high violent crime rate, the other with relatively low rates of violence. One would expect the high-violence nation to have much higher incarceration levels, so looking at rates alone gives a false sense of each country's inclination to punish.

The better yardstick is time served for each type of crime, though even by this measure Europe probably is a lot less punitive. I say probably because European data on time served is hard to come by, and I had to resort to data from 1980 to 1999. To facilitate comparison I used statistics for the United States from the same time period, but as this was a time of increasing punitiveness in the U.S., we were at a disadvantage. I also included Canada and Australia because of their cultural and economic resemblances to the United States.

AVERAGE TIME SERVED IN MONTHS BY COUNTRY AND

CRIME TYPE, 1980–1999[17]

Country	Homicide	Rape	Robbery	Assault
England and Wales	88.33	34.05	18.00	6.66
Sweden	86.95	15.41	15.20	3.07
Australia	120.33	50.91	36.20	23.08
Scotland	94.70	36.40	17.60	7.00
Canada	72.39	—	25.90	27.95
Switzerland	46.16	25.14	20.50	10.13
Netherlands	69.20	15.80	12.14	4.91
Euro Average	82.58	29.62	20.79	11.83
United States	113.63	59.78	41.60	23.40

As is obvious, the European averages, except for homicide, are roughly half of those of the United States. Next I will explain why our punishments are harsher than those of Europe.

* * *

The United States has some very compelling reasons for keeping people in prison—based on circumstances that simply don't exist in other countries. When we factor in these considerations, the United States doesn't look nearly as punitive.

Three key influences on American incarceration rates are recidivism, guns, and murder. These factors generate longer sentences, which in turn raise rates. The longer prisoners serve (all other things being equal) the higher the incarceration rates over time. This is because rates are based on an annual snapshot of the number of inmates (after counting discharges and new entries during the year), and long-term inmates add to the total prisoner count each year until they are released.

WHY LONG-TERM PRISONERS BOOST INCARCERATION RATES

To illustrate the effect of long periods of incarceration on rates, imagine two scenarios involving a jurisdiction with a population of 100,000. (I use 100,000 because rates typically measure events per 100,000). Let's say that 150 offenders are admitted to prison under each scenario. In scenario #1, shorter sentences are more frequent: 100 defendants are sentenced to 2 years while 50 are sentenced to 5 years. Scenario #2 involves longer sentences: 50 defendants get 2 years, 100 receive 5 years. Assume (unrealistic as this is) no additional prisoners are admitted for five years and no inmates are released before serving their full sentences. Now let's compare the annual incarceration rate per 100,000 under each scenario.

Scenario # 1		Scenario # 2	
Year	No. of Prisoners	Year	No. of Prisoners
1	150	1	150
2	150	2	150
3	50	3	100
4	50	4	100
5	50	5	100
AVG:	450/5 = 90		600/5 = 120

In the first two years the incarceration rates are identical: 150 per 100,000 in each scenario. After year 2, however, when the short-sentenced defendants are released, the rates diverge. For years 3 through 5 the rates are double under scenario 2: 100 prisoners out of a general population of 100,000 versus 50 prisoners per 100,000 in scenario 1. Moreover, the average incarceration rate for the five-year period is 33 percent higher under scenario 2 (120 versus 90). In sum, longer sentences mean higher incarceration rates even when the number of admitted prisoners is held constant.

Repeat offending is a fact of life with criminals, and the United States suffered a massive increase in offenders between the 1970s and the 1990s. From 1960 to 1990, violent crime in this country increased 353 percent—perhaps the biggest sustained increase in the nation's history. This led to huge numbers of arrests, convictions, and incarcerations, especially once the criminal justice system was toughened up. From 1960 to 1990, violent crime arrests rose an astounding 407 percent and prison commitments leaped by 271 percent.[18]

During this high crime period, prisoners repeated their offenses many times, both before they were incarcerated and after their release. Once caught and convicted, these repeaters naturally received longer sentences (and did more time) than first offenders, thus boosting imprisonment rates. Consider state prisoners released in 1983: Before their stint in prison, they had been arrested for 1.3 million crimes. Once let out, 63 percent were arrested for new crimes within three years of release. For prisoners freed in 1994, there had been 4.1 million arrests before imprisonment, with 68 percent rearrested within three years of release. In 2005, same story: an average of over ten arrests and five convictions per prisoner before release, with 83 percent rearrested within nine years of discharge, accounting for nearly two million additional arrests.[19]

As you would expect, hundreds of thousands of released ex-prisoners and probationers were re-incarcerated due to new crimes. The latest data (for 2019) reveal that in a single year over 167,000 probationers and parolees failed to comply with the requirements of release and were remanded to state or federal prison.[20] In some states in recent years, two-thirds of prison admissions were parole or probation violators. Some of these violations were technical and led to short sentences that don't add much to imprisonment rates. But many were new crimes, and these repeat offenses generated much longer sentences than comparable crimes by first offenders.[21] Aside from the seriousness of the crime, nothing affects sentencing severity more than the criminal history of the defendant.[22]

The post-1960s crime tsunami led several states to adopt or beef up their habitual offender laws, which increased sentences for recidivating defendants. The objectives were mixed: incapacitate dangerous repeaters, deter them and others from committing crimes, and increase the punishment for incorrigibles. The U.S. Supreme Court upheld such laws, acknowledging the state's public-safety interest in incapacitating and deterring recidivist felons. "Recidivism," the court observed, "has long been recognized as a legitimate basis for increased punishment."[23] Of course, the impact of imposing longer sentences was to raise incarceration rates.

Probably the best known of the repeat offender laws is California's Three Strikes statute, adopted in 1994 (though scaled back in 2012). Under this law a defendant's second strike—a felony conviction preceded by one previous serious or violent felony conviction—resulted in a doubling of the sentence for the second crime (which, before the latest modification of the law, didn't have to be serious or violent). If a convicted felon had two or more serious or violent felony convictions on his record, the sentence for the third felony would be life imprisonment with a minimum term of twenty-five years.[24]

A report on the Three Strikes law concluded that it had "a major effect on the make-up of the prison population" in California. From the law's enactment in 1994 to the end of 2004, the state courts sent over 80,000 second strikers and 7,500 third strikers to prison. By December 2004, nearly 43,000 inmates were serving time under Three Strikes, approximately 26 percent of the total prison population.[25]

Growth in the Three Strikes Inmate Population in State Prison

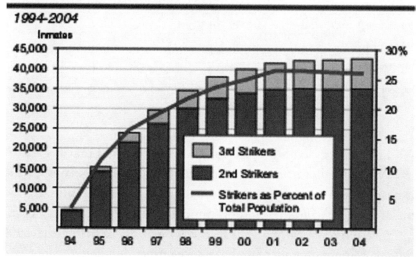

1994-2004

Brown and Jolivette, "A Primer."

Had there been no Three Strikes law, these offenders would have served much shorter sentences and presumably California's incarceration rates would have been lower. By lengthening the terms of imprisonment, habitual offender laws raise incarceration rates.

* * *

Comparable countries—western Europe, Canada and Australia—had far lower crime rates than the United States before the 1990s, far fewer offenders, and therefore way fewer recidivists. U.S. rates were many multiples of the European rates, climbing relentlessly from 1970 to the early 1990s. European rates didn't start to accelerate until the late 1980s and didn't catch up to American levels for another decade—by which time U.S. rates were on the decline.[26]

For homicides, the most accurate crime measure, U.S. crime rates were many multiples of those of the comparable countries.

DECADAL AVERAGE HOMICIDE RATES PER 100,000

	UK	HOLLAND	FRANCE	GERMANY	ITALY	SPAIN	SWEDEN	CANADA	AUSTRALIA	US
1970s	0.9	0.7	0.9	1.2	1.5	0.6	1.1	2.4	1.8	9.4
1980s	1.1	0.9	1.1	1.2	1.8	1	1.3	2.2	2	9.1
1990s	1.2	1.2	1	1.1	2.7	0.9	1.2	1.8	1.8	8.6
Average	1.1	0.9	1	1.2	2	0.8	1.2	2.1	1.9	9

Jan Luiten van Zanden et al. eds., How Was Life?: Global Well-Being Since 1820 (Paris: OECD, 2014), https://doi.org/10.1787/9789264214262-en, 150.

The United States average for the three decades that began with 1970 was nine homicides for every 100,000 of the population, which is nearly seven times the average for the comparable countries. For all major violent crimes (including murder), as well as property crimes, rates were dramatically higher in the United States before the 1990s, though Europe surpassed the U.S. once crime plummeted here.[27]

Data on European recidivism is spotty, but judging by those who are returned to prison—roughly half of those released—the percentages seem comparable to those in the United States. Nevertheless, the radically higher crime rates in the United States before the 1990s would have produced many more prisoners and many more repeat prisoners. The upshot is that recidivism helped make our incarceration rates significantly higher than those of the comparable countries.[28]

***

The second reason for higher incarceration rates in the United States is the widespread use of guns in crimes. Sentences are lengthened for crimes committed with guns, which adds to incarceration rates. Such increases are justified by the fear that gun crimes create, to say nothing of the dangers of victim death or serious injury. Europe and the other comparable countries have nowhere near our level of gun crimes.

Many increased penalties for gun crimes are hidden because the weapon is part of the definition of the offense. Robbery laws are a good example. In New York State, for instance, first degree robbery, a "B" felony, carrying a sentence of five to twenty-five years in prison, is defined as forcible stealing while armed with a deadly weapon or when displaying a loaded firearm capable of being fired. Robbery in the third degree, by contrast, which does not involve a weapon, is a "D" felony, which carries a lesser, two- to seven-year sentence.[29] Armed robbery, in short, adds three years to the minimum sentence for strong-arm (unarmed) robbery and up to eighteen years to the maximum sentence.

In addition to the laws in which gun use is an element of the crime, forty-four states provided, starting in the 1970s, special sentencing enhancements for felonies committed with deadly weapons. Most states added a one-, two-, or three-year mandatory sentence to the penalty for the underlying felony; a substantial number imposed a mandatory five years or more.[30]

Western Europe, Canada, and Australia have far fewer guns and, compared with the United States, far fewer crimes committed with firearms. From 2000 to 2012 there were an estimated 1,500 gun homicides per year in all of Europe, around 20 percent of total homicides. For a comparable period there were nearly 12,000 annual gun homicides in the United States—that's eight times as many as Europe—and guns were responsible for 67 percent of all killings. In 1990, a peak year for murder here, the western European firearm homicide rate was a mere 0.53 per 100,000. The United States rate was 5.57 per 100,000—ten and one-half times higher.[31]

* * *

That brings us to the third reason for our high incarceration rates—murder. Guns play a big role here too since the availability of guns in the United States helps keep our murder rates high. It is, quite simply, easier to kill people, and to kill more people, with a firearm than with a knife or some other weapon requiring hand-to-hand struggle with the victim. This helps explain why the most recent FBI tally revealed that nearly three-quarters of the murders in the United States were carried out with firearms, more than six times the number slain by knives.[32] It also helps explain mass murders, which occur with much greater frequency in the United States than in Europe. In 2019 the United States suffered thirty-one incidents in which four or more people were shot to death. In 2020 the number of mass murder shooting incidents here was twenty-one. Europe had two incidents in 2019, three in 2020.[33]

Since, as we saw, murderers serve long sentences—fifteen years on average—our gun-driven murder rate also drives up our incarceration rates. The long time that murderers spend behind bars is the key. Murder and manslaughter together account for only 2 percent of serious violent crime arrests, but 14 percent of state prisoners. This indicates that although murder does not occur frequently compared with other crimes, the long sentences imposed produce a high proportion of prison inmates.[34]

* * *

Up to now I've been talking about people in prison without mentioning the large numbers of jail inmates—around 734,500 nationwide on any given day. Don't jails contribute to "mass incarceration"? Of course, jails incarcerate, but they don't incarcerate for very long. Jails are the way stations of the criminal justice system; the jail inmate is a transient. Each week an average 53 percent of the inmate population turns over: bunches of new inmates come in; scads more are set free. Two-thirds of jail inmates had been arrested only a day or two earlier. They're awaiting their initial court hearings, after which they usually are released immediately. One-third were already found guilty and were sentenced or are waiting for their sentencing hearing. The crimes of this latter group are often serious, and if so, they probably are on their way to prison.[35]

Jails are horrid, and a jail stay, however short, is still punishment. But length matters. The average jail stay is only twenty-six days, though even that figure is misleading, as it includes the inmates who were just arrested and will be released in a few days, along with those already convicted and sentenced. By the most recent count (2019), there were over 10.3 million jail admissions in a year. But the average daily jail population is under 742,000.[36] Where do all those missing millions go? Most go home (or back to the streets) long before the year is out, and the rest, a minority, go to prison. Given the size of the intake, jails are, in a sense, the epitome of "mass" incarceration, but given the brevity of the stay, they surely are mass incarceration "lite."

The following formula quantifies the difference in length of detention between prisons and jails:

Number of Inmates × Average Time Served (in days) ÷ 1,000,000 = Detention Days per Million
Prison: 1,430,800 × 986 days ÷ 1,000,000 = 1,411[37]
Jail: 734,500 × 26 days ÷ 1,000,000 = 19[38]
1,411 ÷ 19 = 74

As you can see, prisons are responsible for over 74 times more incarceration days per inmate than jails.

The issues for jails and prisons are very different. Prisons raise the question of the amount of punishment appropriate for someone adjudged guilty of a serious crime: Are too many such convicts imprisoned for too long? Is their treatment appropriate to the goals of punishment? Jails raise a different question. Given the lack of trials or pleas for most inmates, the short stays, and the relatively minor infractions, jails lead us to ask whether there should be any confinement at all. Currently, this involves four issues: (1) whether unadjudicated persons should ever be incarcerated; (2) whether more arrested persons can safely be released instead of jailed; (3) whether we've overcriminalized "victimless" activities, such as drug possession; and (4) whether arrest and jail are appropriate for homeless defendants with psychoses or addictions.

Regarding the first issue: No society can afford to release all or even most arrested persons. The risk to the public from more crime and the likelihood of flight from justice simply are too great. This means that thousands will be confined, if only briefly, without a determination of guilt. While everyone can agree that the innocent shouldn't be punished, in *United States v. Salerno*, the Supreme Court rightly distinguished punishment and administrative confinement.[39] This may sound like legal smoke and mirrors; after all, iron bars are iron bars. But what choice is there? Who should assume the risk, the public or the arrestee? Jailing the "innocent"—more accurately, the unadjudicated—is a necessity, especially when the crime is serious and the evidence of guilt is significant.

Issue number two is more nuanced. It asks whether *more* arrestees can be released instead of jailed. This is playing out currently as the "bail reform" issue. Multiple jurisdictions are trying to navigate between public safety and the integrity of judicial processes on the one hand, and individual freedom and its benefits on the other. So far it has been a bumpy road. New York State, for example, adopted a law mandating release of arrestees alleged to have violated numerous felonies and most misdemeanors—even where some of the crimes are violent or the defendant has a long record of failures to appear. Opposition to the law led the state legislature to backtrack, at least partially, only three months after the enactment went into effect.[40] Chicago took a different tack, adopting an algorithm intended to enable the safe release of certain arrestees, but initial analysis indicates that the releases caused an increase in crime.[41]

Issue three involves decriminalization of certain offenses, which would eliminate arrests and jail time for selected violations. A variation is to maintain the prohibition but substitute a ticket or summons for arrest. Debates are underway over the legalization of marijuana, a policy that could significantly reduce arrests for drug possession, thereby thinning jail populations. Likewise up for discussion is whether jail is appropriate for other minor offenses, such as driving with a revoked license. A common thread in this discourse is the conflict between knock-on effects (such as driving accidents or escalation from marijuana to hard drugs), and freedom to engage in activities that don't directly harm others. Another issue is the dearth of workable alternative enforcement mechanisms. What, for instance, can be done short of incarceration with defendants who are released and fail to show up for their court hearings or don't pay fines and court fees?

Finally (issue 4), much thought is being given to the best way to handle the homeless, especially when they are mentally ill or substance addicted. Is arresting and briefly jailing them for loitering and "quality of life" offenses the best way to deal with this problem, or are there treatment modalities that would be more effective? Is it time to be thinking about reopening psychiatric hospitals instead of leaving psychotics on the streets?

These public policy conversations are healthy. But they are not about long-term punishment in prison. Jail controversies are really debates over the best way to handle low-level crimes, especially public order offenses. The issue is the use of the criminal justice system to address such problems and the effectiveness of the alternatives.

* * *

The assertion that the United States cruelly overpunishes lawbreakers is one of those fact-free myths of the contemporary era. It is based on misplaced compassion for repeat offenders who murder, maim, rob, and otherwise abuse their victims, many of whom are low-income minorities.

The truth is that nearly one out of three convicted *felons* (not misdemeanants) and close to one out of four *violent* offenders are released without ever spending time in prison. And for those convicts who are imprisoned only around one in five serves full terms. All told, prisoners serve an average two years and seven months; four years, eight months if the crime was violent.

Historically, by American standards, this is hardly cruel. Neither is it racist. Is it more punitive than other, comparable, countries? Yes. But these nations don't have recidivism rates like ours. They don't have gun crimes anywhere near United States levels. The frequency of their murders, a crime that swells incarceration rates, is far lower than ours.

This isn't to say that we can learn nothing from European prisons. Certainly, the prisons in Scandinavia and Germany are far less dreadful than ours. They focus much more on rehabilitation and reintegration. But America is not Norway, and never will be. We must cope with enormous numbers of violent criminals, and size matters. New York State alone has nearly 30,000 prisoners convicted of violent felonies, whereas the entire Norwegian prison population totals a mere 3,400.[42] Serious comparisons of the United States and other countries are tricky and must move past surface indicators, such as incarceration rates.[43]

In any event, United States imprisonment rates are already in decline; they are as low as they have been in the last two and one-half decades. So long as we remain in a crime trough, this situation undoubtedly will continue, as the public will not demand a toughening of the system. (Ironically, however, this softening may help produce high crime rates.) The one thing we do not need is arbitrary incarceration reductions without regard to public safety. That would be a sure road to injustice for lawbreakers, and more crime for the rest of us.

11

DECARCERATION?

THE MODERN PRISON is now two hundred years old, but no one seems to be celebrating the anniversary. Its critics are legion. Leftists think too many inmates are locked up for too long, or that, in the hyperbolic words of congresswoman Alexandria Ocasio-Cortez (D-NY), prisons are America's "apartheid."[1] Conservatives think they are too costly. Libertarians decry the bloated criminal code and convictions without proof of criminal intent. Everyone agrees that prison does a terrible job at rehabilitating inmates, or in contemporary parlance, "reintegrating" them into society. Just look at our incredibly high recidivism rates.

Some individuals and organizations have called for massive and arbitrary reductions in the prison and jail population, without regard to crime rates.[2] Some are going well beyond reductions in incarceration. They seek full-fledged abolition—an end to prisons altogether! Prison abolition has become a Progressive rallying cry, but aside from a handful of far left Progressives, abolition has not exactly caught on. Some leftist advocates, such as Black Lives Matter cofounder Patrisse Cullors, support abolition but don't expect rapid change. "We're not going to just be able to get rid of prisons in one day, overnight. This is going to be a process." Yes, and a very long process indeed, partly because many abolitionists link the end of prisons to left-wing dreams of social change, including the elimination of war, racism, poverty, homelessness, and alleged lack of opportunity. As the reliably left *Nation* magazine explains, "Abolitionists don't stop at the prison walls . . . They aim to reshape our society as a whole." This pie-in-the-sky Progressivism will not win many adherents among the American public.[3]

It isn't even clear why the abolitionists believe that all the evils on their list must be eradicated before prisons can be eliminated. Perhaps they have adopted a simplistic syllogism in which crime is the product of poverty and racism, and once these are eliminated, a crime-free world will follow. And of course, if there's no crime, who needs prisons? However, the actual relation between war, racism, poverty, and crime is much more nuanced than the ideologues think, as American history demonstrates.[4]

In any event, even if we reject the crude left-wing analysis, there is a huge problem with the abolitionist agenda that its advocates haven't addressed in any meaningful way, perhaps because they don't want to have this conversation. Simply put, if crime will not be abolished or sharply diminished in the near future, what will replace incarceration?

The Left has flirted with so-called restorative justice (RJ) as an alternative,[5] but its inadequacies are glaring. Restorative justice calls for a meeting of crime victims and perpetrators under the direction of a trained facilitator. The aim is to arrive at a way for the perpetrator to make the victim feel whole again, or at least acknowledge his or her pain.

This certainly has its place, but it will not replace imprisonment. For low-level offenses, such as harassment or minor theft, restorative justice may be effective. But offenders like this are usually put on probation, so the benefits in terms of reducing incarceration are insignificant. Restorative justice also could be helpful in campus "date rape" situations where the "he said, she said" evidence prevents clear findings of responsibility. RJ could provide a more satisfying outcome for the female complainant than conventional criminal justice approaches.

For most serious crimes, however, especially crimes of violence, RJ may be useful, but only as a supplement to incarceration. Not only are serious offenders a danger to the community who must be incapacitated, but their crimes are such that the public's sense of justice requires punishment. Retribution may be out of favor with Progressives, but it is an essential ingredient in every criminal justice system. It requires that the punishment be proportionate, that it "fit" the crime. Meetings with victims certainly will not satisfy the public that justice for rapists, robbers or attempted murderers is being served. It won't be adequate for nonviolent prison inmates either, such as gun law violators, drug dealers, drunk drivers, burglars, or major thieves. For the first two (probably the first three) there is no victim with whom to make amends. For the last two, restitution (paying back the stolen property) might be more desirable to victims than statements of regret.

Restorative justice has other problems too. What is to be done with the offender who has no remorse, doesn't want to engage with or help the victim, or just plays the game to avoid incarceration? And what if the victim isn't interested in sitting down with the perpetrator? RJ is a nonstarter in these situations.

Clearly, whatever the benefits of restorative justice, it will not reduce the prison population by 39 percent or anything close. It is likely to be most effective with probationers, who have committed crimes that are sufficiently nonthreatening so that the defendant can be released instead of incarcerated. But this is a population that is already unconfined, so RJ won't help reduce real-world incarceration.

Restorative justice also may be useful with parolees, especially those who have matured in prison and regret their crimes. Unfortunately, this seems to be a small minority of ex-offenders since more than eight of ten parolees commit new offenses while released and are rearrested.[6] Nevertheless, there probably is little disadvantage in giving a parolee the opportunity for atonement, especially since he already will have served his time.

No, restorative justice will not end so-called mass incarceration. It scarcely will make a dent in the prison population.

* * *

Decarcerationists also have offered plans to reduce incarceration by outright releasing prisoners and changing sentencing laws to provide greater leniency going forward. A 2016 report of the Brennan Center for Justice advocates a frightening 39 percent reduction in prison inmates, which comes to the release of 576,000 prisoners.[7] To achieve this the Center recommends a 25 percent reduction in sentences for *the most serious offenses*: murder, robbery, drug trafficking, aggravated assault, burglary, and weapons offenses.[8] (Rape is not included in this list, but there is no explanation for this. Could there have been fear of backlash from feminists and Progressives for proposing the early release of rapists?)

In addition to the early release of the worst offenders, the report advocates *the elimination of imprisonment altogether* for what the authors consider "lower-level" crimes. These offenses include drug possession and "minor" drug trafficking, "lesser" burglary, simple assault, and fraud, forgery, or theft of property valued at up to $10,000.[9]

Although the report is intended as guidance for states wishing to reduce incarceration, the chances of obtaining public support for such sweeping leniency for offenders, especially those committing some of the most reprehensible crimes, are slim to none.

Why would we want such extreme decarceration anyway? According to the Brennan Center, there are two reasons. First, prison is "counterproductive": it "may make some people *more* likely to commit crimes after release," and besides, "alternatives to incarceration promote public safety more effectively."[10]

The second reason offered is race bias. Incarceration, the report says, "drives and reinforces deep seated racial inequity and disproportionately punishes African Americans."[11]

Both claims are specious. Take the contention that imprisonment doesn't promote public safety. It certainly is true that once released, prisoners commit many additional crimes, but whether they'd do fewer crimes if they were imprisoned *less* is a matter of debate. A recent study of federal inmates found the opposite. Offenders incarcerated for more than 120 months (ten years) were approximately 30 percent less likely to recidivate relative to a comparison group receiving less incarceration.[12]

But even if prisons are criminogenic (crime producers), they provide benefits in incapacitation that the report ignores. Simply put: while they're in prison, convicts can't victimize anyone outside. And the earlier the release, the greater the opportunity to reoffend. Once prisoners are discharged, they don't take long to return to crime. Eighteen percent are sent back to prison within six months. Half are returned to their cells within three years.[13] Consequently, if they are released early with their 25 percent Brennan Center discount, thousands more people will become crime victims. And here we are talking about the most serious criminals: murderers, robbers, drug traffickers, aggravated assault perpetrators, and so forth.

The other piece of the Brennan Center proposal—to eliminate imprisonment altogether for so-called low-level crimes—would help spur a new crime wave and would almost certainly set off a public revolt. First, some of these crimes may not be low-level in fact. To get a conviction in a case with proof problems (say, a shaky or compromised witness, or evidence obtained through illegal search), prosecutors often accept pleas to reduced versions of a crime. But the incident that actually occurred may have been much more serious than the plea suggests.

Second, the report's version of "minor" is not likely to be the average citizen's. The report's $10,000 cap on thefts would create open season for car theft or expensive bicycle larcenies. Imagine if thieves knew they would not face prison for stealing your car? I don't think the public would stand for this. Proposals like this suggest that advocacy groups like the Brennan Center are totally out of touch with the American public.

The Center's report claims that the alternatives to incarceration, such as drug, alcohol, and mental health treatment, are more effective in protecting the public.[14] Such interventions may be appropriate in certain cases. Obviously, some addicts benefit from substance abuse treatments. Frequently, however, such interventions fail.[15] When they do succeed, it is often due to the threat of incarceration. As three experts observed, "diversion" programs (removing offenders from the usual criminal processes) and drug treatment courts "rely on the threat of prison as a lever to secure treatment entry, retention, and compliance."[16] Eliminate that threat and you remove the incentive to successfully complete the treatment. Ironically then, following the report's recommendation to abolish imprisonment for relatively minor crimes would make the incarceration alternatives less likely to succeed.

It also is a fact that while the most serious criminals do the most damage and are feared the most, the low-level offenders, especially thieves and burglars, have some of the highest recidivism rates.[17] The ones who go to prison are not there because we indiscriminately punish the really bad along with the not-so-bad. They are imprisoned because they have repeated their crimes many times, and we don't know what else to do with them. If imprisonment is no longer available as an option (and we don't adopt the advanced technologies discussed in chapter 12), society will have little means of coping with such crime. In effect, the public will be handcuffed while thieves and burglars run free.

The Brennan Center's second argument is, essentially, that prisons are racist. This claim is based on the disproportionate number of African Americans in prison, around 38 percent of the inmates, or three times the proportion of the black population of the United States.[18] But however much left-wing advocacy groups like to slide over it, there is a huge difference between racial disparity and racial bias. No group is distributed evenly across all human endeavors; otherwise, each of our professional athletic teams would be around 60 percent non-Hispanic white.

The Brennan Center report offers no proof that bias is responsible for the racial disparity among prisoners. After decades of analysis empirical studies find that the main reason African Americans are disproportionately imprisoned is because they disproportionately violate the laws that lead to incarceration. Furthermore, when blacks receive longer sentences, it is primarily due to the reprehensibility of the crime and their criminal history. As a thorough review of the literature puts it, "considering all the evidence, it seems reasonable to conclude that *the racial disproportionality in the prison population results to a large extent from racial disparities in criminal involvement* but to some extent from racial discrimination at various stages in the criminal justice process."[19]

In any event, the Brennan Center's proposals would be unlikely to reduce the proportion of blacks in prison. Take their suggestion to remove all low-level drug offenders from prison and reduce the prison time of major traffickers. As I observed earlier (in the discussion of Michelle Alexander's work), if all African American drug offenders were removed from prison tomorrow, inmates of color would still be 38 percent of the prison population, which is their current proportion.

We should not despair that the racial disparities of United States prisons are a permanent situation. As people of color make their way up the social ladder, an inevitability in post–civil rights America, they, like the Irish and Italian immigrants before them, will engage in less and less violent crime.[20]

12

E-CARCERATION

IT IS HIGHLY UNLIKELY that crime will decline further in the United States anytime soon. If that is the case, can incarceration still be reduced? Should it? The case for decarceration is not very persuasive, but the political pressures to proceed with it anyway are mounting. However, proposals to aggressively reduce incarceration are risky. Shorter or fewer prison sentences mean more serious criminals on the streets. Given the enormous recidivism rates of released inmates, this is dangerous. Bail reform really means more arrested offenders freed instead of jailed. This too is hazardous, though probably not as risky as early release from prison.

What we need is a system to protect the public *and* reduce incarceration. In this chapter I will propose a way to achieve both these goals with electronic monitoring (EM) of parolees, probationers, and pretrial detainees. As electronic monitoring technology improves, we even may be able to replace traditional incarceration with e-carceration. That prospect is a long way off right now, but it isn't unimaginable.

The technology already exists to electronically satisfy many of the aims of incarceration. Job one, of course, is protection of the public from additional crimes by the offender (including protecting the offender's family and acquaintances, not just strangers). Criminologists call this "incapacitation." Second is "general deterrence," discouraging crime by others because they're scared of being caught and punished. Third, we want retribution, or justice: a punishment that is proportionate to the offense. The punishment must be commensurate with the harm caused. Fourth is "rehabilitation" or reform of the offender. A law-abiding and socially productive ex-offender doesn't recidivate, so reintegration into society—if it can be attained—reduces victimization and incarceration.

E-carceration can achieve some of these goals, not all. But traditional incarceration is not perfect either. There is a big debate over incapacitation (hence, this book): Does our current system of incarceration provide too much, too little, or just the right amount of incapacitation? Whatever the answer, one thing is clear: nothing (short of death) incapacitates like jail or prison. So long as an offender is confined, he or she cannot harm anyone outside the prison walls.

General deterrence has always been a matter of dispute among criminologists, with many arguing that fear of arrest and punishment is low on the list of disincentives to crime, especially for impulsive youth.[1] This argument is put forth despite compelling evidence that the get-tough policies during the crime tsunami years helped significantly reduce crime.[2] In any event there currently is no more effective deterrent than incarceration, especially given the unacceptability of corporal punishment and the contemporary hostility to the death penalty.

As for retribution, differences of opinion mainly relate to the appropriateness of the death penalty, or to life without parole, especially for young offenders, or to the use of long-term solitary confinement. In addition, some Progressives think that certain nonviolent offenders don't deserve to be punished, though the public is unlikely to agree.

Finally, whether we can effectively rehabilitate has been a matter of sharp disagreement for at least a century. Given the enormously high levels of recidivism of ex-prisoners, there is little confidence that prison can reform. But the current alternatives—probation, parole, drug and mental health treatments—have a mixed record at best.[3] When it comes to recidivism, e-carceration is the most promising new development in the field of penology.

In short, imprisonment is better than any other punishment (other than the death penalty) for incapacitation, general deterrence, and retribution. Can e-carceration match these benefits? Right now, the honest answer is no. But e-carceration is going to keep getting better as the technology improves.

***

E-carceration is built around proven tracking technology, the global positioning system (GPS), familiar to millions of drivers who use their mobile phones for traffic and location information. This technology is widely used by government and industry in the United States and is already applied at scale to offenders in Europe. It has countless business applications, such as to package delivery companies, taxi and limousine services, and cargo vessels. Even vital infrastructure and national security operations, including power grids, air traffic control, and military operations, have become dependent on GPS.

GPS technology is already being utilized to monitor offenders in the United States. A Pew survey found that the use of electronic tracking devices by criminal justice agencies rose nearly 140 percent in ten years. More than 125,000 people were supervised with such devices in 2015, and all fifty states, the District of Columbia, and the federal government now use them.[4] But surprisingly—for a country virtually wedded to technology—current use is a drop in the bucket given the size of the offender population.

The electronic monitors used to track the location and movement of offenders have three main components: a GPS receiver, cellular circuitry to communicate with the monitoring agency, and a rechargeable battery.

Refinements such as a miniature speaker and a microphone are also usually added. These components are housed in a waterproof plastic case attached to the offender's ankle with a rubber strap. The newest batteries last for about sixty hours before a recharge is necessary. If the offender attempts to remove the bracelet or tamper with it, or fails to recharge the battery, an alert is sent to the agency that is monitoring the device.

Since the bracelet can track an offender's whereabouts, it can be programmed to deter access to locations that are off-limits and encourage the subject to present himself at places to which he should report. For example, monitoring software can demarcate certain no-go areas—geofenced exclusion zones—such as a crime victim's or a prosecution witness's residence or workplace, or a playground or schoolyard. The device can then caution the offender with an alarm if he nears the prohibited area and alert the authorities should he physically breach the boundary. Once an offender enters the geofenced area, the GPS tracker can transmit his location and the time of entry. This protocol would, for instance, provide protection for an offender's wife/girlfriend or child if they had been the victims and the offender had been directed to stay away from them as a condition of release. Without electronic monitoring the offender is, as a practical matter, on his honor to keep away from his victims. True, he has a parole officer, but dozens of other parolees have the same officer. The bracelet provides a much-needed insurance policy against noncompliance.

Second, geofenced *inclusion* zones, such as a drug treatment clinic, an educational or training facility, or a place of employment, can be created to remind the subject of his obligations. The reminders can be audibles from the GPS device, which contains software programmed to serve the particular requirements of each monitored person. The device can be programmed to announce where and when the subject is supposed to go. The subject will then be able to check in on arrival, perhaps at an electronic kiosk located within the facility. A bracelet would work especially well with an offender sentenced to home confinement. The apartment or house would be geofenced, and the offender would not be able to leave the premises without setting off an alarm and alerting the authorities.

E-carceration also can be used to detect an offender's proximity to known crimes in the area as an aid to investigation. Since GPS reveals the movement of the subject, along with a time and date stamp, the authorities can geomap crimes in an area, say, in a one-day period, and determine whether the subject was present at the crime scene at the time of the offense. They then can interview the individual to see if he may have been involved in the incident.[5]

* * *

The great advantage of e-carceration is its low cost and effectiveness in reducing recidivism. That's why its principal use, at least initially, should be with parolees and probationers: offenders who have been released from prison (paroled) or sentenced to "community corrections" (probation) instead of prison. As things stand now, parolees and probationers are virtually on their honor to conform to the conditions of release because parole and probation officers have too many cases to devote much time to any one of them. With e-carceration, however, there will be a full-time, 24/7 electronic officer minding each offender. The monitoring isn't perfect, as I'll explain, but it's way ahead of the honor system presently in effect.

Electronic monitoring (EM) has been proven to reduce recidivism. A Florida study supported by the U.S. Justice Department and involving over five thousand medium- and high-risk offenders placed on electronic monitoring over a six-year period, found that approximately one in three would have gone to prison had it not been for the monitoring.[6] Needless to say, anything close to a one-third reduction in incarcerations with such a population is a tremendous success: for the individuals involved as well as the public interest in reducing imprisonments while preventing crime.

The success of EM has been demonstrated in countries all over the world, including the UK, numerous European nations, Australia, Israel, and Canada. Several studies using careful scientific analysis have shown that monitoring reduces the likelihood of reoffending when compared with unmonitored release.[7]

Europe is way ahead of us in the use of e-carceration. In England and Wales, there were ninety thousand monitoring orders in 2012, and in France, twenty thousand offenders were tagged (braceleted) in 2015—29 percent of all convicted persons. France uses EM with defendants facing sentences of one year or less, the equivalent of our misdemeanors. The results have been encouraging. Even after controlling for numerous factors that might have affected the outcome, EM was found to have reduced the probability of reconviction between 9 and 11 percent.[8]

There is little doubt that the monitored subject is better off than a prison inmate. He can engage in activities, including travel (though not unrestricted travel), that the prisoner cannot. He is not subject to the routine of the jail or prison, or to the noise, boredom, regimentation, fear, or social isolation of an incarcerative facility. He can return to his home, family, and friends. In a profound sense, the released-though-monitored inmate has his societal life restored. The monitored probationer or pretrial detainee (someone arrested and released after a day or two) avoids that loss of societal life from the start.

Naturally, electronic monitoring is not without shortcomings. E-carceration is intrusive and restricts individual freedom. This is unavoidable. Any intervention that monitors an individual, requiring him to wear and charge a device and to report his location to government authorities, is, by definition, an imposition on freedom. To determine if the intrusion is justified, however, the proper criterion is not whether the monitored subject is less free than the unmonitored, but whether he is freer than the incarcerated. The subject is, after all, a known offender, either arrested for a crime or arrested, adjudicated, and sentenced. He already spent time in jail and maybe in prison as well. By law he could be reincarcerated. Such individuals, especially the ones found guilty and sentenced, must be prepared to forfeit some of their freedom, as is required of all probationers and parolees.

A second problem with an e-system is the lack of sufficient man-power to monitor the software as it reports violations. As more offenders are subject to e-carceration, probation or parole officers and their support staffs may find it increasingly difficult to handle this task along with their other responsibilities. The solution is to provide dedicated staff to monitor the reports, or, in really big jurisdictions, to outsource this responsibility. Monitoring can be contracted out to private companies similar to those that monitor home burglar alarm systems. The monitoring company can report to the probation and parole authorities immediately upon a detected violation and then generate daily and weekly reports on all of the monitored persons in a jurisdiction, with red flags for violations. Outsourcing will add to the expense of e-carceration. But if it is effective in reducing traditional, and expensive, incarceration, that will offset the added cost.

Perhaps the biggest shortcoming of electronic monitoring is that the bracelet cannot determine if the subject is committing another crime. Indeed, even if he triggers the monitoring software, say, by entering a no-go zone, the system can only note and report the breach; it cannot prevent or describe it in detail. Obviously, EM is not as effective as imprisonment, which prevents the violation in the first place. Incapacitation by e-carceration, in other words, is not totally effective when compared with traditional incarceration. But the day may come—sooner than you might think—when technology can resolve this problem too.

A proper cost-benefit analysis makes a strong case for e-carceration. Given the benefits in incapacitation compared with the unmonitored parolee or probationer, the much-reduced expense compared with prison, and the gains in freedom for the offender compared with incarceration, e-carceration must be judged a major breakthrough in penology.

Treatment	Incapacitation	General Deterrence	Retribution	Rehabilitation/ Reintegration	Freedom/ Lack of Restraint	Cost
Prison	✓✓	✓	✓	👎	👎	👎
Unmonitored release	👎	👎	👎	?	✓✓	✓
E-carceration	✓	👎	👎	✓	✓	✓

* * *

Despite its many benefits to offenders when compared with incarceration, electronic monitoring has prompted opposition from left-wing advocacy groups and left-oriented judges. The Electronic Frontier Foundation, for instance, claims that EM imposes "excessive surveillance on people coming home from prison . . . [and] hinders their ability to successfully transition back into the community." However, they provide no proof for the dubious proposition that released prisoners who aren't monitored reintegrate better than monitored offenders. Additionally, the EFF claims that "there is no concrete evidence that electronic monitoring reduces . . . recidivism," despite the numerous studies to the contrary discussed in this chapter.[9]

As for the judiciary, we can expect numerous challenges to EM primarily based on the Fourth Amendment to the Constitution, which prohibits "unreasonable" searches and seizures. The United States Supreme Court already has declared, in *Grady v. North Carolina* (2015), that a state conducts a "search" under the Fourth Amendment "when it attaches a device to a person's body, without consent, for the purpose of tracking that individual's movements."[10] The justices did not say whether such a search is reasonable by Fourth Amendment standards, leaving that decision, at least initially, to the lower courts. But the *Grady* case will open the door to litigation that seeks to impose major restrictions on electronic monitoring.

It should be kept in mind, however, that the Supreme Court has frequently held that probationers and parolees have diminished Fourth Amendment rights, which will provide powerful support for the braceleting of such offenders. "This Court has repeatedly acknowledged," the justices declared, "that a State's interests in reducing recidivism and thereby promoting reintegration and positive citizenship among probationers and parolees warrant privacy intrusions that would not otherwise be tolerated under the Fourth Amendment."[11] So, for example, the Court has upheld the search of a probationer's home without a warrant or probable cause. And it approved the search of a parolee's person even without reasonable suspicion.[12] However, these cases did not involve electronic monitoring, so the question of Fourth Amendment rights in that context remains unanswered.

Despite the Supreme Court's rulings that probationers and parolees have limited rights, some state courts have been throwing up Fourth Amendment obstacles to EM, based mainly on privacy intrusion arguments.

Massachusetts, with one of the most liberal state supreme courts in the country, has thwarted attempts by the state legislature to apply electronic monitoring even to sex offenders unless a judge finds that each particular defendant is at risk of reoffending.[13] But the criminal justice system has a terrible track record for predicting recidivism by sex offenders—70 percent are arrested for a crime after discharge from prison and they commit three times as many rapes and sexual assaults as all other released prisoners[14]—so the court seems to be demanding the impossible. And why should the public assume the risk that a sex offender might reoffend when he could be constrained without incarceration?

The court's answer is that electronic monitoring is too great an imposition. "The GPS device burdens liberty in two ways," the state jurists said, "by its permanent, physical attachment to the offender, and by its continuous surveillance of the offender's activities."[15] This is inaccurate and ominous for the future of EM in Massachusetts. The device was not "permanent" since it was attached only for the duration of the defendant's probation period, six years in this case. Nor did it surveil the defendant's activities; it only monitored his location, revealing nothing about the nature of his activities.

Not all courts are troubled by long-term—even lifelong—monitoring. In this next case a federal court upheld lifetime electronic monitoring of a defendant who had served his full sentence and was released without conditions. *Balleau v. Wall* was decided unanimously in 2016 by the Seventh Circuit Court of Appeals,[16] with an opinion written by the highly respected conservative judge Richard Posner, who took a very different position from the Massachusetts judges regarding the legality of EM.

Following his second conviction for child sexual assault (the first involving an eight-year-old boy; the second a nine year-old girl), Michael Balleau was paroled after serving six years in prison. However, his parole was revoked after he admitted to having continuing fantasies of sex with children. Balleau was then civilly committed for treatment as a sexually violent person and released after five years.[17] Four years before his discharge, Wisconsin had enacted a law requiring that persons released from civil commitment for sexual offenses wear a monitoring device twenty-four hours a day for the rest of their lives. This law was applied to Balleau, who claimed Fourth Amendment and ex post facto violations.[18]

The court, 3-0, rejected both claims. Judge Posner's opinion explained.

> Having to wear a GPS anklet monitor is less restrictive, and less invasive of privacy, than being in jail or prison, or for that matter civilly committed, which realistically is a form of imprisonment. The plaintiff argues that because he is not on bail, parole, probation, or supervised release, and so is free of the usual restrictions on the freedom of a person accused or convicted of a crime, there is no lawful

basis for requiring him to wear the anklet monitor. But this misses two points. The first is the nature of the crimes he committed—sexual molestation of prepubescent children. In other words the plaintiff is a pedophile, which, as the psychologist who evaluated him explained, "predisposes [the plaintiff] to commit sexually violent acts. . . . It is well understood in my profession that pedophilia in adults cannot be changed, and I concluded that Mr. Balleau had not shown that he could suppress or manage his deviant desire."[19]

In short, just because an offender is in the community but not on probation or parole does not mean it is unconstitutional or inappropriate to monitor him. This is especially the case with pedophiles, who are unable to control their desire for sex with children.

Judge Posner's second point is that the impact of the monitoring statute on Balleau's privacy is "slight." This is especially so given that Wisconsin makes sex offenders' criminal records and home addresses public, and private websites such as Family Watchdog enable anyone to determine if a sex offender lives nearby.

"So the plaintiff's privacy has already been severely curtailed as a result of his criminal activities," Posner added,

and he makes no challenge to that loss of privacy. The additional loss from the fact that occasionally his trouser leg hitches up and reveals an anklet monitor that may cause someone who spots it to guess that this is a person who has committed a sex crime must be slight. For it's not as if the Department of Corrections were following the plaintiff around, peeking through his bedroom window, trailing him as he walks to the drug store or the local Starbucks, videotaping his every move, and through such snooping learning (as the amicus curiae brief of the Electronic Frontier Foundation would have it) "whether he is a weekly church goer, a heavy drinker, a regular at the gym, an unfaithful husband," etc.[20]

Not only is the burden on privacy slight, it must be balanced against the gain to society from monitoring persons convicted of "very serious crimes such as sexual offenses against minors, and especially very serious crimes that have high rates of recidivism." Someone convicted of such crimes, therefore, has a diminished expectation of privacy, the standard for Fourth Amendment protection, whether or not he is on probation or parole.[21]

As to the ex post facto claim, Judge Posner addressed it as follows.

A statute is an ex post facto law only if it imposes punishment. . . . The monitoring law is not punishment; it is prevention. . . . The plaintiff does not quarrel with his civil commitment; even though it took away his freedom and was in most respects indistinguishable from confining him in prison, it was not ex post facto punishment because the aim was not to enhance the sentences for his crimes but to prevent him from continuing to molest children. In *Kansas v. Hendricks*, 521 U.S. 346, 368-69, 117 S.Ct. 2072, 138 L.Ed.2d 501 (1997), the Supreme Court held that civil commitment of sex offenders who have completed their prison sentences but are believed to have a psychiatric compulsion to repeat such offenses is not punishment as understood in the Constitution; it is prevention. The aim of the anklet monitor statute is the same, and the difference between having to wear the monitor and being civilly committed is that the former measure is less likely to be perceived as punishment than is being imprisoned in an asylum for the criminally insane. So if civil commitment is not punishment, as the Supreme Court has ruled, then *a fortiori* neither is having to wear an anklet monitor.[22]

With the legal battle lines drawn, one can only hope that common-sense views like Judge Posner's will prevail over the positions of judges who seem eager to raise legal barriers to our best chance for reduced incarceration, reintegration of offenders, *and* protection of the public. Eventually, of course, this issue will have to be resolved by the United

States Supreme Court. The Court currently has a majority said to be conservative, but predicting case outcomes or the voting records of justices is treacherous business.[23]

* * *

Present-day technology, used to reveal the subject's location, has a significant limitation: monitoring cannot determine when the subject is committing a crime. However, according to Mirko Bagaric, dean of Swinburne Law School in Melbourne, Australia, and associates, the technology already exists to monitor offender behavior, not just location.[24] If true, this could be a game-changer for penology.

Behavior monitoring requires three components: a body sensor harness, a stable and secure communication system, and a remote signal processing system that can recognize unauthorized prisoner behavior. The sensor harness must be capable of capturing video and audio signals from the subject's environment and transmitting them to the monitors. This type of sensor unit is already widely used in the United States in the form of body cameras for police officers. These "cop cams" transmit audio and video signals that are stored remotely. For offenders the signals would be monitored in "real time," that is, as the events are occurring. As noted earlier, this would require dedicated monitoring personnel.[25]

The harness would have to operate and be worn at all times, 24/7, which creates some difficulties. First, the sensor would have to function at nighttime with minimal light. However, current technology can support night vision. Second, there may be activities, such as swimming or bathing, that may not be perfectly compatible with a harness. However, as the sensors are made smaller and more water-resistant, this issue should be readily resolved. A third shortcoming is the possibility that the monitored offender simply could attach the harness to another person. Dean Bagaric suggests that this could be resolved by having an upward-facing camera that captures the face of the subject and transmits it continuously. With highly accurate facial recognition software, the monitoring agents can be assured that the wearer is the subject offender, not a stand-in.[26]

Dean Bagaric and colleagues also maintain that technology exists to determine in real time if the subject is committing a crime or engaging in other proscribed misconduct. He points out that self-driving cars also rely on environmental sensors and are capable of operating a vehicle "more safely than any human," a feat that only a few years ago "was seen as a virtually impossible task, and one that was expected to take decades to achieve." "We are now," the writers add, "at the same inflection point in a range of signals processing fields that can be applied to technological incarceration."[27]

Indeed, a recent paper at a technology conference reported the development of a deep learning model for suspicious behavior detection by CCTV, capable of identifying abuse, burglary, the setting off of explosives, shooting, fighting, shoplifting, arson, robbery, stealing, assault, and vandalism.[28] A body cam worn by an offender also would be able to detect and identify such misconduct.

These technological achievements would mark a milestone in offender monitoring, as the subject's misbehavior could be reported directly to the police. (Of course, this would require coordination with police dispatch systems.) In other words, e-carceration would not only provide location information; it would inform the monitoring agents or the police when the subject was violating the law, and it would do so at the time the misconduct was occurring.

This creates, Bagaric and associates point out, yet another possibility that aligns e-carceration more closely with its predecessor, traditional incarceration. They propose incorporating a remote CED, a conduct energy device, such as a stun gun or a Taser, into the electronic bracelet attached to the prisoner's ankle. "If they [monitored offenders] attempt to escape, commit harmful acts, or disable or remove their body sensors," Bagaric and colleagues suggest, "the computers monitoring the events will instantly activate the CEDs embedded in their ankle bracelets to administer the electric shock. This will incapacitate offenders until the arrival of law enforcement officers, whom the computer system will have alerted."[29] Activation of the electric shock could be done automatically when the misconduct is detected, or by human agents assigned to monitor the detection system.

Given such capacity to immobilize, e-carceration approaches parity with incarceration in terms of the treatment of offenders. In fact, Bagaric and coauthors urge, e-carceration actually would be superior to old-fashion iron bars. "Technological incarceration can achieve all of the benefits of conventional imprisonment, and it has a number of additional advantages," they assert. "Not only can it attain the two justifiable objectives of imprisonment—proportionate punishment of offenders and community protection—but it is more economical and humane than conventional incarceration."[30]

The authors then offer this bold conclusion:

> Offenders would suffer less brutality and almost certainly reoffend at a lower rate than at present, thereby increasing public safety. The community would save billions of dollars. Implemented properly, the proposals in this Article could result in the total closure of all but a fraction of existing prisons, saving vast amounts of money and greatly reducing human suffering. The only offenders who would continue to be accommodated in conventional prisons would be offenders who breach the conditions of technological confinement—for example, by escaping or committing serious offenses—and offenders who have committed the most serious offenses, which are equivalent to capital offenses in states that have the death penalty. The latter group of offenders constitute less than five percent of the current prison population.[31]

The contention that current technological capabilities would permit nearly 95 percent of all prisoners to be freed seems more than a bit aspirational at this point. There are likely to be far too many glitches to make anything near such a claim. It is, however, highly probable that we will be able to rely on e-carceration more and more, especially as the monitoring technology improves. As this occurs, we can take additional steps to reduce incarceration and protect the public. These steps are simple, they rely on already available technology that has been proven effective, and they will reduce criminal justice costs.

* * *

It is time for a plan—a realistic, cost-saving plan that actually benefits offenders, reduces incarceration, and protects crime victims, prosecution witnesses, and the general public. The plan calls for the application of electronic monitoring to vastly greater numbers of parolees, probationers, and pretrial detainees. Parolees and probationers have been adjudicated guilty and are, as the data show, most likely to commit additional crimes. Since they already are in the community, my proposal creates no additional public risk. To the contrary, electronic monitoring discourages further criminality, yet substitutes for incarceration and allows offenders to remain with their friends and families, hold down jobs, and achieve crime-free reintegration.

We also should monitor certain pretrial detainees, even though they have not yet been proven guilty. If a defendant has a record of numerous arrests, especially for serious crimes, or repeated failures to show up for court hearings, he ordinarily would be offered bail or sent to jail. In states adopting bail reform proposals, however, many of these defendants are simply set free, creating public risk. A better idea would be to empower the judges to release them with ankle bracelets. For a monitored pretrial defendant, tracking would end when he shows up for all of his court hearings, culminating in his trial (or more commonly, his plea hearing). This usually takes less than a year, depending on backlogs in the jurisdiction.

This plan would create three options for handling pretrial detainees: jail for the most dangerous, outright release for the least dangerous, and monitored release for those in between. Properly administered, EM could herald the end of money bail, long a target of the Left.

Parolees should be first in line for monitoring since they have committed the most serious crimes and are the most likely to recidivate. As we saw earlier, 84 percent of state prisoners are serving time for crimes of violence; serious property crimes, such as burglary or major theft; or "victimless" offenses, such as drunk driving or weapons violations.[32] When they are released before completing their sentences, as eight out of ten are, the overwhelming majority commit more crime. Each year over 125,000 parolees fail to meet the requirements imposed on them when they are given the benefit of early release from prison. Over 111,000 are returned to prison or jailed annually; another 14,000-plus abscond or fail for some other reason.[33] Eight of every ten parolees reoffend after release, accounting for nearly two million arrests.[34]

Given the dangerousness of this population, monitoring technology should be applied to nearly all parolees as a condition of release. In most cases the tracking will continue for the duration of the unserved portion of the sentence. The most recent data indicate that parolees will face about three years and nine months of monitoring on average, with an extra seventeen months for violent offenders.[35] However, with pedophiles and other high-risk offenders, monitoring for life may be required.

Probationers are another population that would benefit from electronic monitoring. After a determination of guilt, they are released to the community in lieu of imprisonment, subject to various conditions (community service, no drugs, no guns, show up for court hearings, etc.). These requirements should be easy to satisfy, but they are unevenly enforced by overworked probation officers. Each year roughly 414,000 probationers fail to meet their obligations and over 294,000 are reincarcerated.[36] Given this enormous washout rate, monitoring probationers would provide immense benefits. Ordinarily, such monitoring would continue until the probation period expires, usually from one to three years (though the probation period could last longer for some high-risk defendants). E-carceration would enable more probationers to remain in their communities and reduce the likelihood that they would reoffend, which in turn would keep them out of jail or prison and improve their chances of rehabilitation.

Though some judges seem to think that EM compromises the Fourth Amendment rights of parolees and probationers, such claims should be repudiated. The Supreme Court has repeatedly recognized that parolees and probationers have diminished rights. As the justices stated, "a State's interests in reducing recidivism and thereby promoting reintegration and positive citizenship among probationers and parolees warrant privacy intrusions that would not otherwise be tolerated under the Fourth Amendment."[37] This principle should be applied in the electronic monitoring situation.

To summarize: we ought to be applying electronic monitoring to parolees, probationers, and many pretrial detainees. The additional expense of doing so—more equipment, more personnel to monitor the subjects—would be more than offset by reductions in the cost of jailing or imprisoning offenders. Plus, we would be sparing more offenders the pains of incarceration, allowing them to return (or remain) in their communities with their friends and families, and incentivizing them to conform to the law and reintegrate into law-abiding society. Yet we would achieve all this without creating more risk for the public. Keep in mind that electronic monitoring is for offenders who are already in the community and are essentially unmonitored.

* * *

Two centuries ago, with the development of the penitentiary, the United States was in the vanguard of criminal justice reform. Europeans, such as Alexis de Tocqueville, came here to see how punishment could be done more humanely yet more effectively. Now, in the twenty-first century, we no longer are confident that our justice system is either fair or effective. Many think that Europe is way ahead of us, especially in the use of electronic monitoring with offenders. We are, however, still among the global leaders in technology. It is time to take advantage of our expertise and apply the latest in electronic technology to the justice system.

Vastly expanding electronic monitoring will require strong political support, but for astute politicians, the advantages should be clear. E-carceration will reduce traditional incarceration and promote offender reintegration, pleasing the Left. It will at the same time reduce recidivism, protect the public, and save money on prisons, giving satisfaction to the Right. Plus, serious and violent criminals will continue to be imprisoned; we will not be, despite left-wing pipe dreams, shutting down our prisons anytime soon. That should allay the fears of the general public. E-carceration is one of those rarities in criminal justice—a win/win plan for the public and offenders.

A SELECTIVE BIBLIOGRAPHY

Readers interested in fine points should see the notes accompanying each chapter. For more general exploration of issues pertaining to punishment or penology, see the following.

HISTORY OF PUNISHMENT IN THE UNITED STATES

Friedman, Lawrence M. *Crime and Punishment in American History.* (New York: Basic Books, 1993).

Walker Samuel. *Popular Justice: A History of American Criminal Justice.* 2nd ed. (New York: Oxford, 1998).

Though a bit dated, these two books still provide valuable comprehensive histories of punitive practices in the United States. Friedman also discusses the history of crime.

DATA ON CRIME AND PUNISHMENT IN THE CONTEMPORARY PERIOD

For current-day crime and incarceration data, nothing compares with the Bureau of Justice Statistics of the United States Department of Justice. Go to their website at https://bjs.ojp.gov/ and search on any topic of interest.

State governments also provide data. For example, New York at https://www.criminaljustice.ny.gov/ (click on "Statistics"), or California's "Open Justice" portal, https://openjustice.doj.ca.gov/data.

CAPITAL PUNISHMENT

The best history of the death penalty in the United States is Stuart Banner, *The Death Penalty: An American History* (Cambridge, MA: Harvard University Press, 2002). Unlike most discussions, Banner's has no agenda.

ORIGINS OF THE PENITENTIARY

Though it focuses on New York State, W. David Lewis, *From Newgate to Dannemora: The Rise of the Penitentiary in New York, 1796–1848* (Ithaca, NY: Cornell University Press, 1965), is a good source for the birth of the prison in the United States.

CONVICT LEASE

Douglas A. Blackmon, *Slavery by Another Name: The Re-Enslavement of Black Americans from the Civil War to World War II* (New York: Anchor Books, 2008), is a disturbing account of the punishment of African Americans in (mainly) the late nineteenth century.

PRISONS IN THE TWENTIETH CENTURY

Many fine articles are collected in Norval Morris and David J. Rothman, *The Oxford History of the Prison: The Practice of Punishment in Western Society* (New York: Oxford, 1995). Especially useful is Edgardo Rotman, "The Failure of Reform: United States, 1865–1965" on pages 151–77.

The best account of prison farms in the Jim Crow era is David M. Oshinsky, *"Worse Than Slavery": Parchman Farm and the Ordeal of Jim Crow Justice* (New York: Free Press, 1996).

On progressivism in penology I recommend David J. Rothman, *Conscience and Convenience: The Asylum and Its Alternatives in Progressive America* (Boston: Little, Brown, 1980), and Edgardo Rotman's "The Failure of Reform," in *The Oxford History of the Prison,* cited above.

For the post–World War II period, see Blake McKelvey, *American Prisons: A History of Good Intentions* (Montclair, NJ: Patterson Smith, 1977).

The influence of judges on prison reform is covered by Malcom M. Feeley and Edward L. Rubin, *Judicial Policy Making and the Modern State: How the Courts Reformed America's Prisons* (Cambridge, UK: Cambridge University Press, 1998).

MASS INCARCERATION

There's an enormous literature on this subject, which you can track with Google and Google Scholar, but nearly all the books and articles have an anti-imprisonment (if not anti-America) agenda.

A comprehensive view is presented by Jeremy Travis, Bruce Western, and Steve Redburn, eds., *The Growth of Incarceration in the United States: Exploring Causes and Consequences* (Washington, DC: National Academies Press, 2014). Be warned, though, that the impact on imprisonment of the great post-1960s crime wave is damagingly underplayed.

An empirically grounded work that challenges many of the Left's dogmas is John F. Pfaff, *Locked In: The True Causes of Mass Incarceration and How to Achieve Real Reform* (New York: Basic Books, 2017).

ACKNOWLEDGMENTS

I got wonderfully helpful advice from three colleagues at (or formerly at) John Jay College of Criminal Justice: Dorothy Schulz, Professor Emerita in the Department of Law, Police Science and Criminal Justice Administration; Robert D. McCrie, Professor and Deputy Chair, Department of Security, Fire, and Emergency Management; and James P. Levine, Professor Emeritus and Dean of Research at the College.

Each of the three spent hours reading my manuscript, spotting sins of omission and commission, and making excellent suggestions for improvement. That they didn't always agree with my analysis or my proposals is a tribute to them—they helped me anyway—and a lesson for those who have lost sight of one of the great benefits of the university: the interaction of those with opposing views.

It deeply saddens me to add that several months after helping me Jim Levine passed away. Jim was a dear friend, a wonderful colleague, and an excellent scholar. I dedicate this volume to his memory.

I also want to express my gratitude to those who helped with some of the statistical material in the book. Peter E. Kretzmer, former Senior Economist at the Bank of America, advised on a portion of my statistical analysis. Jie Xu, Assistant Professor of Criminal Justice at St. John's University, helped me collect some key data. And E. Ann Carson, Statistician at the federal Bureau of Justice Statistics, was always responsive to my inquiries.

Thanks as well to Todd E. Humphreys, Associate Professor of Aerospace Engineering, The University of Texas at Austin, for his expertise on certain technical aspects of GPS.

Some of the material in chapter 10 was previously published on the Law & Liberty website, especially at https://lawliberty.org/forum/anincarceration-nation/. I appreciate the republication permission from Richard Reinsch, editor of the website.

Of course, without the dedication of the editorial and production team at Republic Book Publishers this volume never would have graced the bookshelves.

I owe so much to my dear Sandra, whose advice and encouragement have been essential to all of my work. Fortunately for me she considers lifelong love and devotion adequate recompense.

NOTES

INTRODUCTION

1   U.S. Department of Justice, Bureau of Justice Statistics, *Prisoners in 2019* (2020), reports 1,430,800 state and federal prisoners at year-end 2019. U.S. Department of Justice, Bureau of Justice Statistics, *Jail Inmates in 2019* (2021), states that there were 734,500 jail inmates at midyear 2019. Combined, there were 2,165,300 incarcerated individuals in the United States.

2   U.S. Department of Justice, Bureau of Justice Statistics, *Felony Sentences in State Courts, 2006 – Statistical Tables* (2009), table 1.2.

3   U.S. Department of Justice, Bureau of Justice Statistics, *Criminal Victimization, 2019* (2020), tables 1, 2.

4   FBI, *Uniform Crime Reports 2019*, tables 1, 29. A portion of the arrests were for crimes that occurred in previous years.

5   U.S. Department of Justice, Bureau of Justice Statistics, *Prisoners in 2019*, table 8 (data for calendar 2019). U.S. Department of Justice, Bureau of Justice Statistics, *Impact of COVID-19 on the Local Jail Population, January-June 2020* (2021), app table 10 (data for June 30, 2018 through June 30, 2019).

6   U.S. Department of Justice, Bureau of Justice Statistics, *Time Served in State Prison, 2018* (2021). The average time served by all state prisoners released in 2018, from initial admission to initial release, was 2.7 years, and the median time served was 1.3 years.

CHAPTER 1: MAIM AND SHAME: COLONIAL ERA PUNISHMENTS

1   Juliet Haines Mofford, *"The Devil Made Me Do It!": Crime and Punishment in Early New England* (Guilford, CT: Globe Pequot, 2011), 57.

2   Lawrence M. Friedman, *Crime and Punishment in American History* (New York: Basic Books, 1993), 32.

3   Kathryn Preyer, "Penal Measures in the American Colonies: An Overview," *American Journal of Legal History* 26, no. 4 (October 1982): 327.

4   Some colonies had workhouses or "houses of correction," which could be considered forerunners of the prison. But these institutions were not for ordinary criminals and didn't punish for a predetermined period of time. They confined, at forced labor, vagrants, idlers, paupers, fortune-tellers, runaways, and common drunkards. Friedman, *Crime and Punishment in American History*, 49.

5   Friedman, 49–50.

6   Preyer, "Penal Measures in the American Colonies," 334.

7   Benefit of clergy began in England in the High Middle Ages as a protection of clergymen against trial by temporal, as opposed to ecclesiastical, courts. As few laymen could read, proof of literacy was, at first, the test for the benefit. Soon literate non-clergy began to assert the claim, which the authorities granted to laypersons, but just once per accused. To prevent repeat claims (which real clergy were permitted to make), the offender was branded on the hand or thumb so there would be proof that the benefit had already been used. By the time the American colonies adopted the benefit, it had become a reprieve for first-time capital offenders: they were branded instead of executed. By the late eighteenth century, it was abolished in most of the United States. Stuart Banner, *The Death Penalty: An American History* (Cambridge, MA: Harvard University Press, 2002), 62–64.

8   Bradley Chapin, *Criminal Justice in Colonial America, 1606–1660* (Athens, GA: University of Georgia Press, 2010), 8.

9   Banner, *The Death Penalty*, 24, 46–47.

10   Preyer, "Penal Measures in the American Colonies," 346.

11   Philip J. Schwarz, *Twice Condemned: Slaves and the Criminal Laws of Virginia, 1705–1865* (Baton Rouge: Louisiana State University Press, 1988), 15, table 1.

12   Preyer, "Penal Measures in the American Colonies," 334.

13   Preyer, 339; A. Roger Ekirch, "Bound for America: A Profile of British Convicts Transported to the Colonies, 1718–1775," *William and Mary Quarterly* 42, no. 2 (April 1985), 188.

14   "Forty stripes he may give him, and not exceed: lest, if he should exceed, and beat him above these with many stripes, then thy brother should seem vile unto thee" (Deuteronomy 25:3, King James Version). Subsequently, Jewish Torah commentary (Mishnah, Maccoth, fol. 22, 10) and Christian scripture (2 Corinthians 11:24) set the number at thirty-nine to avoid exceeding forty by mistake.

15   Preyer, "Penal Measures in the American Colonies," 335, 337, 344.

16   Mofford, *"The Devil Made Me Do It!,"* 10.

17   Friedman, *Crime and Punishment in American History*, 38–39.

CHAPTER 2: THE SILENT TREATMENT: BIRTH OF THE PENITENTIARY

1   The population rose elevenfold, from an estimated 250,888 in 1700, to 2,780,369 in 1780. U.S. Census Bureau, *Bicentennial Edition: Historical Statistics of the United States, Colonial Times to 1970* (1975), Series Z 1-19, p. 1168, https://www.census.gov/library/publications/1975/compendia/hist_stats_colonial-1970.html.

2   Rush, who was enormously influential in medicine, education, politics, and criminal justice in the United States, was supportive of the Quakers but was himself a Presbyterian, and from his forties on, a member of the Episcopal Church. David Freeman Hawke, *Benjamin Rush: Revolutionary Gadfly* (Indianapolis: Bobbs-Merrill, 1971), 272–73, 311.

3   Louis P. Masur, *Rites of Execution: Capital Punishment and the Transformation of American Culture, 1776–1865* (New York: Oxford University Press, 1989), 82.

4   The term *penitentiary* suggests a facility to encourage repentance, but there was no general agreement in the late eighteenth century that prisons would or could achieve this. The term replaced "hard labor house" in 1778 in the writings of English penal reformers William Eden, William Blackstone, and John Howard. Whether 1778 marks the first time "penitentiary" was used in print isn't clear, but the term was adopted in the English Penitentiary Act of that year, drafted by Eden and Blackstone. Michael Ignatieff, *A Just Measure of Pain: The Penitentiary in the Industrial Revolution, 1750–1850* (New York: Pantheon Books, 1978), 47, 94.

5   Ignatieff, 82–83, 86. Rex A. Skidmore, "Penological Pioneering in the Walnut Street Jail, 1789–1799," *Journal of Criminal Law & Criminology* 39, no. 2 (1948): 167–80.

6   Gustave de Beaumont and Alexis de Tocqueville, *On the Penitentiary System in the United States, and Its Application in France; with an Appendix on Penal Colonies, and Also, Statistical Notes*, trans. Francis Lieber (Philadelphia: Carey, Lea & Blanchard, 1833), https://archive.org/details/onpenitentiarysy00beau-uoft/page/n6/mode/1up?q=Section+II.

7   Charles W. Dean, "The Story of New-Gate," *Federal Probation* 43 (1979): 8–14, 12.

8   Dean, 13.

9   W. David Lewis, *From Newgate to Dannemora: The Rise of the Penitentiary in New York, 1796–1848* (Ithaca, NY: Cornell University Press, 1965), 29–32.

10   Lewis, 34–35, 37, 40–41, 43, 46, 50.

11   Lewis, 46.

12   Lewis, 92, 118–20.

13   Lewis, 84.

14   Lewis, 68–70.

15   Lewis, 232–34.

16   Lewis, 268–70, 272.

17   Lewis, 252, 256–67.

18   U.S. Bureau of Justice Statistics, *Time Served in State Prison, 2018* (see intro., n. 6); Prison Association of New York, *Third Report of the Prison Association of New York, Part I* (New York: Burns & Baner, 1847), 150, 204. Eighty percent of Auburn inmates served sentences between two and five years. This seems to have been typical of the mid-nineteenth century. A study of prisons in Pennsylvania, Massachusetts, Ohio, and Wisconsin over several decades found that 81 percent of the entering inmates served five years or less. The authors also found pardons in about 15 percent of the cases, which is very high by present-day standards, but understandable in an era without "good time" release or parole. E. C. Wines and Theodore W. Dwight, *Report on the Prisons and Reformatories of the United States and Canada, Made to the Legislature of New York, January, 1867* (Albany: Van Benthuysen & Sons, 1867).

19   Blake McKelvey, *American Prisons: A Study in American Social History Prior to 1915* (Chicago: University of Chicago Press, 1936), 57–68.

CHAPTER 3: BLACK GULAG: CONVICT LEASE

1   Douglas A. Blackmon, *Slavery by Another Name: The Re-Enslavement of Black Americans from the Civil War to World War II* (New York: Anchor Books, 2008).

2   Blackmon, 100; Matthew J. Mancini, "Race, Economics, and the Abandonment of Convict Leasing," *Journal of Negro History* 63, no. 4 (1978): 341.

3   Edward L. Ayers, *Vengeance and Justice: Crime and Punishment in the 19th-Century American South* (New York: Oxford University Press, 1984), 196.

4   Mancini, "Race, Economics, and the Abandonment of Convict Leasing," 349 Blackmon, *Slavery by Another Name*, 101–2, 306.

5   Ayers, *Vengeance and Justice*, 61, 61n57.

6   Schwarz, *Twice Condemned*, 52 (see chap. 1, n. 11). From 1786 to 1865 in Virginia, which boasted the biggest slave population in the United States, there were an estimated 9,100 slave trials and 4,550 convictions. Schwarz, 42.

7   Ayers, *Vengeance and Justice*, 186.

8   Ayers, 188–90.

9   Florida had 125 convicts in 1881, 1,071 by 1904. Mississippi's convict population quadrupled in a mere eight years, between 1871 and 1879. Alabama's convict count was 374 in 1869, 1,183 in 1892, 1,878 in 1903, and 2,453 in 1919. Mancini, "Race, Economics, and the Abandonment of Convict Leasing," 343.

10   Mancini, 343–34.

11   Ayers, *Vengeance and Justice*, 199.

12   Blackmon, *Slavery by Another Name*, 56.

13   Blackmon, 72.

14   Blackmon, 71.

15   Blackmon, 71.

16   Blackmon, 1–2, 66. A study of leasing in Georgia found that prewar sentences were lighter than lease sentences. Prewar, two-thirds of the sentences were from one to four years; under the lease, one-to four-year sentences were around 45 percent of the total. Mancini, "Race, Economics, and the Abandonment of Convict Leasing," 345.

17   Blackmon, *Slavery by Another Name*, 2.

18   Joel Williamson, *The Crucible of Race: Black-White Relations in the American South Since Emancipation* (New York: Oxford University Press, 1984), 58; Ayers, *Vengeance and Justice*, 200.

19   Williamson, 215, 221. Mancini, "Race, Economics, and the Abandonment of Convict Leasing," 348.

20   Blackmon, *Slavery by Another Name*, 176-80, 210–11, 219–20, 231–32, 248, 369. Peonage means compelling someone to labor to pay off a debt. The federal government's authority to prohibit such a practice derived from the Thirteenth Amendment, outlawing slavery or "involuntary servitude." The Supreme Court held that the Thirteenth Amendment, unlike the Fourteenth, may be applied to private individuals. Clyatt v. United States, 197 U.S. 207 (1905).

21   Blackmon, *Slavery by Another Name*, 365, 371; Mancini, "Race, Economics, and the Abandonment of Convict Leasing," 349; Ayers, *Vengeance and Justice*, 222.

CHAPTER 4: PROGRESSIVES

1   Use of "reformatory" in reference to a penal institution traces back at least as far as 1838, when a report in England urged the creation of "juvenile reformatories." Since the report indicated that such facilities already were widely accepted, it is likely that the term was used before 1838. John A. Stack, "Deterrence and Reformation in Early Victorian Social Policy: The Case of Parkhurst Prison, 1838–1864," *Historical Reflections/Réflexions Historiques* 6, no. 2 (Winter/Hiver 1979): 389.

2   E. C. Wines, ed., *Transactions of the National Congress on Penitentiary and Reformatory Discipline* (Albany: Argus, 1871), 541.

3   Wines, 541–46.

4   Friedman, *Crime and Punishment in American History*, 161 (see chap. 1, n. 2).

5   National Commission on Law Enforcement and Observance, *Report on Penal Institutions Probation and Parole, No. 9* [Wickersham Commission] (Washington, DC: U.S. G.P.O., 1931), 127.

6   Nicolette Parisi and Joseph A. Zillo, "Good Time: The Forgotten Issue," *Crime & Delinquency*, no. 2 (1983): 231–32.

7   National Commission on Law Enforcement and Observance, *Report on Penal Institutions Probation and Parole, No. 9*, 130.

8   National Commission on Law Enforcement and Observance, 128.

9   U.S. Department of Justice, Bureau of Justice Statistics, *2018 Update on Prisoner Recidivism: A 9-Year Follow-up Period (2005–2014)* (2018). The study tracked for nine years 67,966 state prisoners released in 2005. Eighty-three percent were rearrested and only 1 percent of the arrests were for a technical violation of the terms of release.

10   David J. Rothman, *Conscience and Convenience: The Asylum and Its Alternatives in Progressive America* (Boston: Little, Brown, 1980), 162, 181; Samuel Walker, *Popular Justice: A History of American Criminal Justice,* 2nd ed. (New York: Oxford, 1998), 165.

11   Rothman, *Conscience and Convenience*, 129.

12   U.S. Department of Commerce, Bureau of the Census, *Prisoners in State and Federal Prisons and Reformatories 1926* (U.S. G.P.O., 1929), table 15, p. 20. Rothman, *Conscience and Convenience*, 194.

13   Friedman, *Crime and Punishment in American History*, 161 (see chap. 1, n. 2). An 1881 New York law was less harsh, as it applied only to first offenses punishable by more than five years, whereupon a second offense was punishable by nothing less than ten. Friedman, 161.

14   Under the modern-day Three Strikes law, a defendant's second strike—a felony conviction preceded by one previous serious or violent felony conviction—resulted in a doubling of the sentence for the second crime. If a convicted felon had two or more serious or violent felony convictions on his record, the sentence for the third felony would be life imprisonment with a minimum term of twenty-five years. The law was subsequently softened by requiring that the second felony also be serious or violent. See ch. 10, n. 23.

15   Elmira opened in 1876, but it took four more years to complete construction, partly because of the use of inexperienced and difficult-to-manage inmate labor. Alexander Pisciotta, *Benevolent Repression: Social Control and the American Reformatory-Prison Movement* (New York: NYU Press, 1996), 13–14. Rothman, *Conscience and Convenience*, 33.

16   Pisciotta, *Benevolent Repression*, 20.

17   Pisciotta, 24.

18   Pisciotta, 127, 142.

19   Carolyn Rebecca Eggleston, "Zebulon Brockway and Elmira Reformatory: A Study of Correctional/Special Education" (PhD diss., Virginia Commonwealth University, 1989), 92.

20   Sheldon Glueck and Eleanor Glueck, *Criminal Careers in Retrospect* (New York: Kraus Reprint, 1967, 1943), 121. Thirty-two percent engaged in serious criminality, and 29 percent committed minor offenses. The Gluecks defined serious crime as felonies, minor crimes as, for example, drunkenness, vagrancy, and family neglect. (p. 133).

21   Pisciotta, *Benevolent Repression*, 22, 152. See also Walker, *Popular Justice*, 170 (see n. 10, above), quoting Pisciotta with approval. Pisciotta relies on the analysis of French philosopher Michel Foucault, who claims that penal institutions are part of a much broader system of social control. Michel Foucault, *Discipline and Punish: The Birth of the Prison*, trans Alan Sheridan (New York: Pantheon Books, 1977). However, neither Pisciotta nor Foucault ever proved that greater social control was sought by reformers who endorsed and campaigned for more humanitarian treatment of criminals.

22   State Board of Managers of Reformatories, *Fortieth Annual Report of the New York State Reformatory at Elmira and the Fifteenth Annual Report of the Eastern New York Reformatory at Napanoch* (New York: Summary Press, 1916), 17.

23   Current-day first offenders in New York convicted of Burglary third degree or Grand Larceny second degree would probably be placed on probation or given some other non-incarcerative sentence. In 2013, according to the Council of State Governments, 80 percent of New York City probationers successfully completed the sentence. Justice Center: The Council of State Governments, "Improving Probation and Alternatives to Incarceration in New York State: Increasing Public Safety & Reducing Spending on Prisons and Jails," February 2013, https://csgjusticecenter.org/wp-content/uploads/2020/02/122112_Probation-ATI-Recs_BRIEF_for-NYSAC.pdf. Note, though it may be purely coincidental, that 80 percent is approximately the same success rate claimed for Elmira over a century ago.

24   Henry Herbert Goddard, *The Kallikak Family: A Study in the Heredity of Feeble-Mindedness* (New York: Macmillan, 1912); Goddard, *Feeble-Mindedness: Its Causes and Consequences* (New York: Macmillan, 1914), 9.

25   Buck v. Bell, 274 U.S. 200 (1927). In an 8–1 decision, Justice Oliver Wendell Holmes wrote for the majority: "It is better for all the world, if instead of waiting to execute degenerate offspring for crime, or to let them starve for their imbecility, society can prevent those who are manifestly unfit from continuing their kind. The principle that sustains compulsory vaccination is broad enough to cover cutting the Fallopian tubes. . . . Three generations of imbeciles are enough." *Buck*, 274 U.S. at 207.

26   Pisciotta, *Benevolent Repression*, 131, 133–34, 137.

27   Eggleston, "Zebulon Brockway and Elmira Reformatory," 182–84. My account of the abuse allegations against Brockway and his resignation was drawn from Eggleston, 182–210.

28   Rothman, *Conscience and Convenience*, 36.

29   Pisciotta, *Benevolent Repression*, 143.

30   Edgardo Rotman, "The Failure of Reform: United States, 1865–1965," in Norval Morris and David J. Rothman, *The Oxford History of the Prison: The Practice of Punishment in Western Society* (New York: Oxford, 1995), 151–77. Rotman points out that Elmira's prisoner count had doubled by the 1890s and that one-third of the inmates "always" were recidivists. Rotman, 174.

31   Barry Latzer, *The Roots of Violent Crime in America: From the Gilded Age through the Great Depression* (Baton Rouge: Louisiana State University Press, 2020), chap. 10. The homicide rate in the 1920s averaged 8.95 per 100,000, and exceeded 9 per 100,000 for six of the ten years. The average rate for the 1980s, a particularly violent recent decade, was 9.2.

32   Margaret Werner Cahalan, *Historical Corrections Statistics in the United States, 1850–1984* (Washington, DC: GPO, 1986), table 3–8.

CHAPTER 5: SOUTHERN REGRESSIVISM

1   Latzer, *The Roots of Violent Crime in America*, chaps. 3–4 (see chap. 4, n. 31).

2   Jesse F. Steiner and Roy M. Brown, *The North Carolina Chain Gang: A Study of County Convict Road Work* (Westport, CT: Negro Universities Press, 1970, 1927), 125. Arrests for minor crimes are discretionary with police, who get little credit for apprehending misdemeanants. But discretion also lends itself to race discrimination.

3   Robert Perkinson, *Texas Tough: The Rise of America's Prison Empire* (New York: Metropolitan Books, 2010), 158–59, 165.

4   Perkinson, 166–7, 169, 174–75.

5   Perkinson, 185–88, 206.

6   *A Summary of The Texas Prison Survey* (Austin[?]: Texas Committee on Prisons and Prison Labor, 1924), 13-16.

7   Perkinson, *Texas Tough*, 197–99.

8   Perkinson, 201–3.

9   Perkinson, 205.

10   Arthur Penn's 1967 film, *Bonnie and Clyde*, starring Faye Dunaway and Warren Beatty, was a smash hit. It depicted the pair as modern-day Robin Hoods, while law enforcement was portrayed unsympathetically. Steven Chermak and Frankie Y. Bailey, eds., *Crimes and Trials of the Century: From the Black Sox Scandal to the Attica Prison Riots*, vol. 1 (Westport, CT: Greenwood Press, 2007), 116, 128; Perkinson, *Texas Tough*, 215.

11   Chermak and Bailey, eds., *Crimes and Trials of the Century*, 119, 122, 125.

12   David M. Oshinsky, *"Worse Than Slavery": Parchman Farm and the Ordeal of Jim Crow Justice* (New York: Free Press, 1996), 1, 109, 110. Oshinsky's book is the principal source for my discussion of Parchman.

13   Oshinsky, 137, 162–63, 180.

14   Oshinsky, 137–39.

15   Oshinsky, 137. People of color received very little education at this time in the South, where spending on schools was much lower than in the rest of the country and spending on black schools was lower still. Bureau of the Census, *The Social and Economic Status Black Population in the United States: An Historical View, 1790–1978*, Current Population Reports, P-23, no. 80 (Washington, DC: Government Printing Office, 1979), tables 63, 68.

16   See "Negro Prison Songs from The Mississippi State Penitentiary," Internet Archive, https://archive.org/details/negroprisonsongs/BlackWomen.wav.

17   Oshinsky, 143–45.

18   Oshinsky, 139, 149–50.

19   Oshinsky, 141, 146, 148, 196. Gates v. Collier, 501 F.2d 1291 (5th Cir. 1974) ended the trusty system and flagrant inmate abuse at Parchman.

20   Oshinsky, 140.

21   Oshinsky, 138, 153–54.

22   Oshinsky, 224.

23   Alex Lichtenstein, "Good Roads and Chain Gangs in the Progressive South: 'The Negro Convict Is a Slave,'" *Journal of Southern History* 59, no. 1 (February 1993): 86.

24   Lichtenstein, 87, 89, 100, 102.

25   Steiner and Brown, *The North Carolina Chain Gang*, 125, 136. It wasn't until 1933 that North Carolina centralized control over its prisoners and abolished convict leasing statewide. Milfred Fierce, *Slavery Revisited: Blacks and the Southern Convict Lease System, 1865–1933* (New York: Africana Studies Research Center, Brooklyn College, CUNY, 1994), 192–93.

26   Lichtenstein, "Good Roads and Chain Gangs in the Progressive South," 93.

CHAPTER 6: THE DECLINE OF DEATH

1   The five-year average refers to 2015 to 2019 inclusive, for which the average was 23.6 executions per year. The ten-year period without executions appears to refer to the years 2011 through November 10, 2020. Death Penalty Information Center, https://deathpenaltyinfo.org/. All states with capital punishment statutes use lethal injection. U.S. Department of Justice, Bureau of Justice Statistics, *Capital Punishment, 2016* (2018).

2   Despite the assiduous work of Watt Espy in compiling comprehensive lists of executions in the United States, there are significant gaps in the count. See Paul H. Blackman and Vance McLaughlin, "The Espy File on American Executions: User Beware," *Homicide Studies* 15, no. 3 (2011): 209–27.

3   Howard W. Allen and Jerome M. Clubb, *Race, Class, and the Death Penalty: Capital Punishment in American History* (Albany: State University of New York Press, 2008), 18. The twentieth-century rate was for the period ending in 1945. However, since fewer executions were carried out in the postwar years (which had no executions at all for eight years, 1968–1976), the rate would not have been higher had those years been included.

4   This change in sensibilities is associated with the growth of the middle class in the United States and may be comparable to a similar long-term change in Europe. The classic expression of this gradual change in sensibilities is found in Norbert Elias, *The Civilizing Process: Sociogenic and Psychogenic Investigations* (Oxford, UK: Blackwell, 1994, 1939).

5   On death penalty procedures see Barry Latzer and David McCord, *Death Penalty Cases: Leading U.S. Supreme Court Cases on Capital Punishment*, 3rd ed. (Boston: Butterworth-Heinemann), 24–33. Kennedy v. Louisiana, 554 U.S. 407 (2008), prohibits the execution of child rapists where the victim did not die and death was not intended.

6   Banner, *The Death Penalty*, 10–13 (see chap. 1, n. 7).

7   Banner, 90–91, 98.

8   Allen and Clubb, *Race, Class, and the Death Penalty*, 19, 21. Throughout the nineteenth century black execution rates (including slaves and free persons of color, irrespective of region) were eight times the rate or more of all U.S. whites. Allen and Clubb, 21. The discrepancy is attributable to leniency toward whites who killed, the execution of blacks for certain race-based crimes, and the high conviction rates of blacks who killed whites. As to the latter, Schwarz found that in sixty-six trials of slaves accused of killing whites in Virginia (1706–85), 81 percent were convicted, but in trials of slaves for killing other slaves, 52 percent were convicted. Schwarz, *Twice Condemned*, 46 (see chap. 1, n. 11).

9   Virginia, with the largest slave population in North America, compensated slave owners for lawful executions from 1705 on. However, private executions by slave owners and slave suicides or flight to avoid such executions were not compensated. Allen and Clubb, 20, 52–53.

10   From 1882 to 1930 there were 2,314 lynchings of African Americans and 1,977 legal executions. Lynchings were 54 percent of the total 4,291 executions. Stewart E. Tolnay and E. M. Beck, *A Festival of Violence: An Analysis of Southern Lynchings, 1882–1930* (Urbana: University of Illinois Press, 1995), 100–101.

11   Ayers, *Vengeance and Justice*, 252–53 (see chap. 3, n. 3). Two-thirds of the black lynchings were for murder, rape, or rape-murder. E. M. Beck and Stewart E. Tolnay, "When Race Didn't Matter: Black and White Mob Violence Against Their Own Color," in W. Fitzhugh Brundage, *Under Sentence of Death: Lynching in the South* (Chapel Hill: University of North Carolina Press, 1997), 132–54, 141.

12   Beck and Tolnay, in Brundage, 202; Tolnay and Beck, *A Festival of Violence*, 239.

13   Banner, *The Death Penalty*, 46–47. Burning at the stake was reserved for slaves who murdered their owners or plotted revolt, and wives who killed their husbands. Banner, 71.

14   Banner, 146–47, 153–55.

15   Banner, 180–82, 184–86, 189, 191–92; In re Kemmler, 136 U.S. 436 (1890).

16   Banner, 196, 198–200, 203.

17   Banner, 297; Baze v. Rees, 553 U.S. 35 (2008). The vote was 7–2, with only Justices Ginsburg and David Souter dissenting.

18   The stronger bias argument is that the death penalty was carried out more aggressively when the murder victim was white, but more infrequently when the victim was black. The Supreme Court took up this issue but found the proof, offered by law professor David Baldus, insufficient to halt the penalty on race discrimination grounds. McCleskey v. Kemp, 481 U.S. 279 (1987). So long as the death penalty is not abolished altogether, the Baldus argument boomerangs against black murderers. Since the killers of African Americans are usually other African Americans, any effort to even the racial score and execute more killers of blacks would mean more executions of blacks.

19   On violent crime see Barry Latzer, *The Rise and Fall of Violent Crime in America* (New York, Encounter Books, 2016), chap. 2; U.S. Department of Justice, Bureau of Justice Statistics, *Capital Punishment, 2018—Statistical Tables* (2020), app. table 4.

20   Furman v. Georgia, 408 U.S. 238 (1972). In Gregg v. Georgia, 428 U.S. 153, 188 (1976), a plurality of the justices said, "While *Furman* did not hold that the infliction of the death penalty per se violates the Constitution's ban on cruel and unusual punishments, it did recognize that the penalty of death is different in kind from any other punishment imposed under our system of criminal justice." I don't see the relationship between the harshness of the death penalty and the acceptability of inconsistency in its imposition. Are life sentences imposed inconsistently more acceptable than death sentences? I don't think so. We accept inconsistencies in punishments because they are inevitable and no justice system could survive if it remitted sentences on such grounds.

21   From 1977 to 2018 the average time between a death sentence and execution was 12 years. In 2018 it was 19.8 years. U.S. Department of Justice, Bureau of Justice Statistics, *Capital Punishment, 2018—Statistical Tables* (2020), table 11. The prejudice problem of a unitary or one-part trial may be illustrated as follows. Suppose the defense attorney wishes to present mitigating evidence that the defendant was badly abused by his father as a child and that this should be taken into account when deciding the sentence. In a unitary trial such evidence might be excluded by the judge out of concern that the jury, out of sympathy, might determine that the defendant was not guilty even though the evidence of guilt was very strong. They might acquit rather than see such an abused defendant face death. In a two-part (or bifurcated) trial, such evidence would be admissible, but only in the second or penalty phase once the jury would, at that point, already have found the defendant guilty.

22   Some may think that death is less cruel than life in prison without parole, but nearly all capital prisoners maintain appeals, which suggests that they would rather live in prison than die.

CHAPTER 7: THE FAILURE OF LENIENCY

1   Heather Ann Thompson, *Blood in the Water: The Attica Prison Uprising of 1971 and Its Legacy* (New York: Vintage, 2016), 559. Thompson, writing from a pro-prisoner perspective, said, "The decade immediately after the Attica rebellion saw vital victories for prisoners across the country in general and at Attica in particular." Thompson, 560. There are discrepancies in the death count at Attica. Thompson reports forty-three dead. Thompson, v. The report of the state commission puts the number at thirty-nine. *Attica: The Official Report of the New York State Special Commission on Attica* (New York: Bantam Books, 1972), 373. The difference may reflect subsequent deaths of people wounded in the retaking of the prison.

2   Latzer, *The Rise and Fall of Violent Crime in America*, 103–263 (see chap. 6, n. 19).

3   Rotman, "The Failure of Reform," in Morris and Rothman, *The Oxford History of the Prison*, 178–79 (see chap. 4, n. 30).

4   Rothman, *Conscience and Convenience*, 380–81, 391–93 (see chap. 4, n. 10).

5   Rothman, 404–18.

6   David Garland contends that a "civilizing process," a term first developed by historical sociologist Norbert Elias, has led to more sympathy for criminals. "The most obvious sense in which the civilizing process may be seen to have affected the penal system is in the extension of sympathy . . . to the offender, a development which has gradually ameliorated the lot of the offender and lessened the intensity of the punishment brought to bear." David Garland, *Punishment and Modern Society: A Study in Social Theory* (Chicago: University of Chicago Press, 1990), 236.

7   Rotman, "The Failure of Reform," in Morris and Rothman, *The Oxford History of the Prison*, 184 (see chap. 4, n. 30).

8   As late as 1963, the Supreme Court of Delaware declined to declare whipping as a sentence to be cruel and unusual punishment. State v. Cannon, 190 A.2d 514 (Del 1963); Oshinsky, *"Worse Than Slavery,"* 149 (see chap. 5, n. 12).

9   Jackson v. Bishop, 404 F.2d 571, 579 (8th Cir. 1968) (Arkansas); Gates v. Collier, 501 F.2d 1291 (5th Cir. 1974) (Mississippi).

10   The Thirteenth Amendment states: "Neither slavery nor involuntary servitude, except as a punishment for crime whereof the party shall have been duly convicted, shall exist within the United States, or any place subject to their jurisdiction."

11   Holt v. Sarver, 309 F. Supp. 362 (E.D. Ark. 1970), a federal court decision condemning the Arkansas prison farm, described the work as follows. "Men assigned to the fields are required to work long hours six days a week, except for a few holidays, if weather permits. They are worked regardless of heat, and summers can be very hot at Cummins; in the winter they are not required to work when the temperature is below freezing, but they are required to work in merely bad or wet weather regardless of the season of the year. The men are not supplied by the State with particularly warm clothing for winter work, nor are they furnished any bad weather gear. There is evidence that at times men have been sent to the fields without shoes or with inadequate shoes. The field work is arduous and is particularly onerous in the case of men who have had no previous experience in chopping and picking cotton or in harvesting vegetables, fruits, and berries." *Holt*, 309 F. Supp. at 370.

12   Rothman, *Conscience and Convenience*, 138, 141–42 (see chap. 4, n. 10).

13   Blake McKelvey, *American Prisons: A History of Good Intentions* (Montclair, NJ: Patterson Smith, 1977), 315.

14   Rothman, *Conscience and Convenience*, 142.

15   Oshinsky, *"Worse Than Slavery,"* 255 (see chap. 5, n. 12).

16   Cahalan, *Historical Corrections Statistics in the United States*, table 3-2 (see chap. 4, n. 32); U.S. Department of Justice, Bureau of Justice Statistics, *Race of Prisoners Admitted to State and Federal Institutions, 1926–86* (1991), table 1.

17   McKelvey, *American Prisons*, 322–27.

18   Robert Martinson, "What Works?—Questions and Answers about Prison Reform," *Public Interest* (Spring 1974): 22–54, 49. Though Martinson didn't title his article "Nothing Works," many thought he had or concluded that that was the main takeaway. Having been published at a time of exceptionally high crime rates, Martinson's work, though criticized by many academics, became a pillar of the "get-tough-on-crime" movement. Martinson himself was a liberal. He committed suicide in 1979.

19   American Friends Service Committee, *Struggle for Justice: A Report on Crime and Punishment in America* (New York, Hill and Wang, 1971), 88–90, 97–99, 144.

20   U.S. Department of Justice, Bureau of Justice Statistics, *Race of Prisoners Admitted to State and Federal Institutions, 1926–86*, table 2. By 1970, nonwhites, who were 12.5 percent of the United States population, were 39 percent of the admissions to state and federal prisons.

21   See, e.g., Cooper v. Pate, 378 U.S. 546 (1964). This case was significant for enabling prisoners to go to federal court to challenge alleged denials of constitutional rights. The facts of the case involved attempts to suppress the Black Muslims in prisons. Cooper, an inmate in the Illinois State Penitentiary, claimed religious discrimination because he was not allowed to obtain a Quran and other Black Muslim publications. The federal court of appeals denied his right to sue, pointing out "certain social studies which show that the Black Muslim Movement, despite its pretext of a religious facade, is an organization that, outside of prison walls, has for its object the overthrow of the white race, and inside prison walls, has an impressive history of inciting riots and violence." Cooper v. Pate, 324 F.2d 165, 166 (7th Cir. 1963). The Supreme Court reversed, opening the door to federal suits by prisoners on First Amendment religious freedom grounds. Cooper's Supreme Court victory made regulation of the Black Muslims by prison officials more difficult by implicitly treating the organization as a bona fide religion and recognizing the right of inmates to obtain its publications.

22   McKelvey, *American Prisons*, 354. The official report on Attica noted the "new kind of inmate," black or Hispanic, who considered himself a political prisoner. *Attica: The Official Report of the New York State Special Commission on Attica*, 106.

23   *Attica: The Official Report of the New York State Special Commission on Attica*, 109, 373; McKelvey, *American Prisons*, 358.

24   Thompson, *Blood in the Water*, 4, 23, 27, 30.

25   McKelvey, *American Prisons*, 353–54.

26   Thompson, *Blood in the Water*, 36, 154; *Attica: The Official Report of the New York State Special Commission on Attica*, 108–9, 251–57, 316–17, 320, 323, 373–74.

27   Thompson, *Blood in the Water*, 2. In a letter to Oswald a few months before the uprising, the five inmates calling themselves the Attica Liberation Faction asserted that New York's prisons had been turned into "the fascist concentration camps of modern America." Thompson, 134.

28   In 1970, nonwhites were 39 percent of the admissions to state and federal prisons. In 1975, African Americans alone (excluding other nonwhites) comprised 35 percent of the admissions, rising to 41 percent in 1980. U.S. Department of Justice, Bureau of Justice Statistics, *Race of Prisoners Admitted to State and Federal Institutions, 1926–86*, table 2.

29   The Supreme Court's decision in Johnson v. California, 543 U.S. 499 (2005), illustrates the tension between desegregation and violence in prisons. A majority of the justices ruled that the Constitution requires that states meet the most demanding legal test for lawsuits alleging race discrimination in prisons. This effectively prohibited racial segregation in prisons. Justice Clarence Thomas wrote in dissent, "California oversees roughly 160,000 inmates, in prisons that have been a breeding ground for some of the most violent prison gangs in America—all of them organized along racial lines. In that atmosphere, California racially segregates a portion of its inmates, in a part of its prisons, for brief periods of up to 60 days, until the State can arrange permanent housing. The majority is concerned with sparing inmates the indignity and stigma of racial discrimination. . . . California is concerned with their safety and saving their lives." *Johnson*, 543 U.S. at 524.

30   See generally, Malcom M. Feeley and Edward L. Rubin, *Judicial Policy Making and the Modern State: How the Courts Reformed America's Prisons* (Cambridge, UK: Cambridge University Press, 1998). The U.S. Supreme Court, itself dominated by activist judges under chief justice Earl Warren, facilitated lawsuits against police, and by implication, corrections personnel, by its decision in Monroe v. Pape, 365 U.S. 167 (1961). *Pape* dusted off a rarely used 1871 law (originally known as the Ku Klux Klan Act, now found in the federal code at 42 U.S.C. §1983) to afford individual citizens a right to sue in the federal courts for deprivations of federally protected rights by persons acting under color of law. Acting "under color of law" meant that an employee of a county or municipality, such as a prison guard, could be sued for allegedly depriving someone of their constitutional rights while carrying out their duties. The Supreme Court subsequently made §1983 suits more lucrative, and therefore more numerous, when it permitted such suits against local governments, not just individual employees. Monell v. Department of Social Services, 436 U.S. 658 (1978).

31   Holt v. Sarver, 309 F. Supp. 362 (E.D. Ark. 1970).

32   *Holt*, 309 F. Supp. at 381.

33   Oshinsky, *"Worse Than Slavery,"* 250 (see chap. 5, n. 12); Friedman, *Crime and Punishment in American History*, 313 (see chap. 1, n. 2); Perkinson, *Texas Tough*, 278 (see chap. 5, n. 3).

34   Ruiz v. Estelle, 503 F. Supp. 1265 (S.D. Tex. 1980); Perkinson, *Texas Tough*, 311.

35   Hudson v. Palmer, 468 U.S. 517 (1984), is an example of a failed effort to expand inmate rights. The Supreme Court held that prisoners have no Fourth Amendment right to privacy in their cells. Random shakedown searches of cells, said the Court, are "the most effective weapon of the prison administrator in the fight against the proliferation of weapons, drugs, and other contraband." Another unsuccessful effort was Jones v. North Carolina Prisoners' Labor Union, 433 U.S. 119 (1977), which stated that prison inmates do not have a right under the First Amendment to join labor unions. In a sense, though, *Jones* shows how lenient the system had become: it took a Supreme Court ruling to deny prisoners a right to unionize.

CHAPTER 8: THE BUILDUP

1   University at Albany, *Sourcebook of Criminal Justice Statistics Online*, http://www.albany.edu/sourcebook/, table 3.106.2012.

2   Hazel Erskine, "The Polls: Fear of Violence and Crime," *Public Opinion Quarterly* 38, no. 1 (1974): 137–38, 140–41.

3   Cf. Katherine Beckett, *Making Crime Pay: Law and Order in Contemporary American Politics* (Oxford, UK: Oxford University Press, 1997), 27, 32, with Peter K. Enns, *Incarceration Nation: How the United States Became the Most Punitive Democracy in the World* (New York: Cambridge University Press, 2016), 65.

4   Nese F. DeBruyne and Anne Leland, *American War and Military Operations Casualties: Lists and Statistics*, Report RL32492 (Washington, DC: GPO, 2015), 2, 3, 5, 12, 17; U.S. Department of Justice, Bureau of Justice Statistics, *Highlights from 20 Years of Surveying Crime Victims: The National Crime Victimization Survey, 1973–92* (1993), 5, 16, 17, 29; U.S. Department of Justice, Bureau of Justice Statistics, *Injuries from Crime* (1989), 3; James Garafolo and L. Paul Sutton, *Compensating Victims of Violent Crime: Potential Costs and Coverage of a National Program* (Albany, NY: Criminal Justice Research Center, 1977), table 11, 30; U.S. Department of Justice, Bureau of Justice Statistics, *Violent Crime* (1994), 3.

5   William J. Collins and Robert A. Margo, "The Economic Aftermath of the 1960s Riots in American Cities: Evidence from Property Values," Vanderbilt University and NBER, May 2004, table 1, 22, accessed November 13, 2011, http://aeaweb.org/annual_mtg_papers/2005/0109_1015_0203.pdf; Stephan Thernstrom and Abigail Thernstrom, *America in Black and White: One Nation, Indivisible* (New York: Simon and Schuster, 1997), 159.

6   Newark lost fifty thousand residents per decade in the 1970s and the 1980s, more than a quarter of the city's population. Brad Parks, "Newark 1967 Crossroads Pt. 3: After the Riots Change Is Slow to Come," *Newark Star-Ledger Blog*, July 10, 2007, http://blog.nj.com/ledgernewark/2007/07/crossroads_pt_3.html. The movement out of the inner city of professional and working-class blacks is discussed in William Julius Wilson, *The Truly Disadvantaged: the Inner City, the Underclass, and Public Policy* (Chicago: University of Chicago Press, 1987), 49–50.

7   U.S. Department of Justice, Bureau of Justice Statistics, *Prisoners in 1990* (1991), table 2.

8   Federal Bureau of Investigation, *Uniform Crime Reports for the United States and Its Possessions* (1950), table 15; Federal Bureau of Investigation, *Crime in the United States, 1960, Uniform Crime Reports*, table 8; Federal Bureau of Investigation, *Crime in the United States, 1970, Uniform Crime Reports*, table 13.

9   Morgan O. Reynolds, "Crime and Punishment in America," National Center for Policy Analysis, policy report no. 193 (June 1995), table A-5, 28, accessed January 6, 2012, http://www.ncpa.org/pdfs/st193.pdf (no longer accessible); Isaac Ehrlich, "Crime, Punishment, and the Market for Offenses," *Journal of Economic Perspectives* 10, no. 1 (1996): 45.

10   Latzer, *The Rise and Fall of Violent Crime in America*, 159, 232 (see chap. 6, n. 19). See also William J. Stuntz, *The Collapse of American Criminal Justice* (Cambridge, MA: Harvard University Press, 2011), 252: "Proof is impossible, but the low and falling prison populations of the 1960s and early 1970s probably contributed to rising levels of serious crime during those years."

11   Cahalan, *Historical Corrections Statistics in the United States, 1850–1984*, table 3-3 (see chap. 4, n. 32); U.S. Department of Justice, Bureau of Justice Statistics, National Prisoner Statistics Program, https://bjs.ojp.gov/data-collection/national-prisoner-statistics-nps-program.

12   For instance, the Supreme Court once struck down a federal law making it a crime to possess a firearm in a school zone. United States v. Lopez, 514 U.S. 549 (1995). The court ruled that Congress had no authority to regulate guns unless they were transported in interstate commerce. Congress amended the law to meet this objection. Gun Free School Zone Act, amended, 18 U.S.C. §922(q)(2)(A) (Supp. IV 1998).

13   Omnibus Crime Control and Safe Streets Act of 1968, P.L. 90-351. From the mid-1980s to the mid-1990s, Congress increased appropriations to state and local law enforcement agencies and enacted five major anti-crime bills: the Crime Control Act of 1984 (P.L. 98-473); the Anti-Drug Abuse Act of 1986 (P.L. 99-570); the Anti-Drug Abuse Act of 1988 (P.L. 100-690); the Crime Control Act of 1990 (P.L. 101-647); and the Violent Crime Control and Law Enforcement Act of 1994 (P.L. 103-322).

14   Total arrests from FBI, *Uniform Crime Reports*, 1970, 1990 and 2000, minus arrests for offenses unlikely to result in imprisonment, viz.: vandalism, prostitution, drunkenness (not including DUI), disorderly conduct, vagrancy, curfew/loitering, runaways.

15   FBI, *Uniform Crime Reports 2018*, https://ucr.fbi.gov/crime-in-the-u.s/2018/crime-in-the-u.s.-2018/topic-pages/clearance-browse-by/national-data. Reported crimes that go unsolved include 86 percent of burglaries, 70 percent of robberies, and 67 percent of rapes.

16   Prosecutors: U.S. Department of Justice, Bureau of Justice Statistics, *Prosecutors in State Courts, 1990* (1992), table 4; *Prosecutors in State Courts, 2001* (2002), p. 4. Indigent defense: U.S. Department of Justice, Bureau of Justice Statistics, *Indigent Defense* (1996), table 2. Judges: Thomas B. Marvell and Paul M. Dempsey, "Growth in State Judgeships 1970–1984: What Factors Are Important?," *Judicature*, no. 5 (February–March 1985): 276; U.S. Department of Justice, Bureau of Justice Statistics, *State Court Organization, 2011* (2013), table 3. Court personnel: *Statistical Abstract 1980*, p. 192, no. 324; *Statistical Abstract 1985*, p. 175, no. 298; University at Albany, *Sourcebook of Criminal Justice Statistics Online*, table 1.21.2006.

17   Cahalan, *Historical Corrections Statistics in the United States, 1850–1984*, table 3-35 (see chap. 4, n. 32); U.S. Department of Justice, Bureau of Justice Statistics, *Census of State and Federal Correctional Facilities, 1984* (1987), table 1; U.S. Department of Justice, Bureau of Justice Statistics, *Census of State and Federal Correctional Facilities, 1995* (1997), iv; U.S. Department of Justice, Bureau of Justice Statistics, *Census of State and Federal Correctional Facilities, 2005* (2008), app table 5.

18   Cahalan, *Historical Corrections Statistics in the United States, 1850–1984*, tables 4-15, 4-19, 4-22 (see chap. 4, n. 32); U.S. Department of Justice, Bureau of Justice Statistics, *Jails and Jail Inmates, 1993–94* (1995), 1. The average stay for jail inmates was twenty-six days. Those convicted of misdemeanors, if not released, could serve up to one year. U.S. Department of Justice, Bureau of Justice Statistics, *Jail Inmates in 2019* (see intro., n. 1).

19   Steven D. Levitt, "Understanding Why Crime Fell in the 1990s: Four Factors That Explain the Decline and Six That Do Not," *Journal of Economic Perspectives* 18, no. 1 (2004): 163–90; Bert Useem and Anne Morrison Piehl, *Prison State: The Challenge of Mass Incarceration* (New York: Cambridge University Press, 2008), 80. William Spelman, "The Limited Importance of Prison Expansion," in *The Crime Drop in America*, ed. Alfred Blumstein and Joel Wallman (Cambridge: Cambridge University Press, 2000), 123.

20   Barry Latzer, "When Biden Was Tough on Crime," *Wall Street Journal*, August 5, 2019.

21   Friedman, *Crime and Punishment in American History*, x–xi (see chap. 1, n. 2).

CHAPTER 9: DENYING THE CRIME TSUNAMI

1   Marie Gottschalk, *Caught: The Prison State and the Lockdown of American Politics* (Princeton: Princeton University Press, 2016), 258; Michael Javen Fortner, *Black Silent Majority: The Rockefeller Drug Laws and the Politics of Punishment* (Cambridge: Harvard University Press, 2015), 22; John F. Pfaff, *Locked In: The True Causes of Mass Incarceration and How to Achieve Real Reform* (New York: Basic Books, 2017), viii; Michelle Alexander, *The New Jim Crow: Mass Incarceration in the Age of Colorblindness* (New York: New Press, 2012); Emily Bazelon, *Charged: The New Movement to Transform American Prosecution and End Mass Incarceration* (New York: Random House, 2019), xxxi.

2   "100 Notable Books of 2016," *New York Times*, Sunday Book Review, December 4, 2016, 24, http://www.nytimes.com/2016/11/23/books/review/100-notable-books-of-2016.html.

3   Jeremy Travis, Bruce Western, and Steve Redburn, eds, *The Growth of Incarceration in the United States: Exploring Causes and Consequences* (Washington, DC: National Academies Press, 2014), 3.

4   Michelle Alexander, *The New Jim Crow: Mass Incarceration in the Age of Colorblindness* (New York: New Press, 2012).

5   Alexander, 102.

6   U.S. Department of Justice, Bureau of Justice Statistics, *Correctional Populations in the United States, 2017–2018*, (2020), table 1. Of 6,522,100 under corrections in 2018, 4,399,000 (67.4 percent) were in the community; 2,123,100 were in prison or jail.

7   There was, however, a 1 percent decrease in the proportion of the correctional population released to the community from 2008 to 2018. This may reflect the pressure on the system to reduce arrests and prosecutions for low-level offenses (such as marijuana possession), the kind that usually lead to a sentence of probation. U.S. Department of Justice, Bureau of Justice Statistics, *Correctional Populations in the United States, 2017–2018*, table 1.

8   U.S. Department of Justice, Bureau of Justice Statistics, *Probation and Parole in the United States, 2017–2018* (2020), app. table 4.

9   Blacks were 31 percent of probationers in 2000, 30 percent in 2015, and 30 percent in 2017–18. U.S. Department of Justice, Bureau of Justice Statistics, *Probation and Parole in the United States, 2016* (2018), app. table 4; U.S. Department of Justice, Bureau of Justice Statistics, *Probation and Parole in the United States, 2017–2018*, app. table 4.

10   For murder, the crime with the most accurate statistics, the African American offending rate averaged 7.7 times the white rate over a thirty-eight-year period, 1976–2014. U.S. Department of Justice, Bureau of Justice Statistics, *Homicide Trends in the United States* (2007).

11   Alexander, *New Jim Crow*, 210.

12   U.S. Department of Justice, Bureau of Justice Statistics, *2018 Update on Prisoner Recidivism*, table 7 (see chap. 4, n. 9). Based on a thirty-state sample.

13   In 2000 African Americans were 40 percent of all parolees; in 2015, 38 percent. U.S. Department of Justice, Bureau of Justice Statistics, *Probation and Parole in the United States, 2016*, app. table 8. In 2018 African Americans were 30 percent of parolees, which may reflect the recent decline in black incarceration. U.S. Department of Justice, Bureau of Justice Statistics, *Probation and Parole in the United States, 2017–2018*, app. table 4.

14   Alexander, *New Jim Crow*, 101, emphasis in original.

15   U.S. Department of Justice, Bureau of Justice Statistics, *Prisoners in 2019*, table 14 (see intro., n. 1).

16   U.S. Department of Justice, Bureau of Justice Statistics, *Prisoners in 2019*, table 14.

17   U.S. Department of Justice, Bureau of Justice Statistics, *Prisoners in 2019*, table 16. Over 99 percent of federal prisoners sentenced for drug offenses were convicted of trafficking, not possession.

18   John F. Pfaff, "Symposium: Drug Policy Reality and Reform; The War on Drugs and Prison Growth: Limited Importance, Limited Legislative Options," *Harvard Journal on Legislation* 52 (2015): 179.

19   U.S. Department of Justice, Bureau of Justice Statistics, *Prisoners in 1994* (1995), tables 14, 11.

20   U.S. Department of Justice, Bureau of Justice Statistics, *Comparing Federal and State Prison Inmates, 1991* (1994), table 4. Fifty-five percent of blacks in federal prison were in for drug crimes, but in 1991 federal prisoners were a mere 7 percent of all inmates. U.S. Department of Justice, Bureau of Justice Statistics, *Comparing Federal and State Prison Inmates, 1991*, iii.

21   U.S. Department of Justice, Bureau of Justice Statistics, *Prisoners in 2019*, table 13 (see intro., n. 1). In 2018, the proportion of prisoners serving sentences for drug violations was: blacks, 12.7 percent; whites, 16.3 percent; Hispanics, 10.5 percent.

22   U.S. Department of Justice, Bureau of Justice Statistics, *Prisoners in 2000* (2001), table 19.

23   Roland Neil and Christopher Winship, "Methodological Challenges and Opportunities in Testing for Racial Discrimination in Policing," *Annual Review of Criminology* 2, no. 1 (2019): 73–98.

24   For the claim that implicit bias explains disproportionate black drug arrests, see Katherine Beckett, "Race, Drugs, and Law Enforcement: Toward Equitable Policing," *Criminology & Public Policy* 11 (2012): 641–53. For analysis approving the deployment hypothesis, see Robin S. Engel, Michael R. Smith, and Francis T. Cullen, "Race, Place, and Drug Enforcement: Reconsidering the Impact of Citizen Complaints and Crime Rates on Drug Arrests," *Criminology & Public Policy* 11, no. 4 (2012): 603–35. The Engel et al. article found that with calls for service as a benchmark, whites, not blacks or Hispanics, were disproportionately arrested for drug crimes. Regarding black fear of crime and demands for tougher law enforcement, see James Forman, *Locking Up Our Own: Crime and Punishment in Black America* (New York: Farrar, Straus, 2017).

25   U.S. Department of Justice, Bureau of Justice Statistics, *Race and Ethnicity of Violent Crime Offenders and Arrestees, 2018* (2021), table 2.

26   Elizabeth Hinton, *From the War on Poverty to the War on Crime: The Making of Mass Incarceration in America* (Cambridge, MA: Harvard University Press, 2016).

27   Hinton, 21–22.

28   Hinton, 21.

29   Edward C. Banfield, *The Unheavenly City Revisited* (Boston: Little, Brown, 1974, 1968), 84.

30   Banfield, 96.

31   James Q. Wilson, *Thinking about Crime*, rev. ed. (New York: Vintage Books, 1985, 1975).

32   Wilson, 108–10.

33   Wilson, 255.

34   Wilson, 256.

35   James Q. Wilson and George L. Kelling, "Broken Windows," *Atlantic Monthly*, March, 1982, 29–38.

36   Black social pathology does not play a significant explanatory role in Wilson's noteworthy writings in the 1980s. In Wilson's and psychologist Richard Herrnstein's major theoretical work on crime, *Crime and Human Nature*, black "cultural pathology" is mentioned in passing in a chapter on race and crime. However, the authors consider the concept subsumed under "inadequate socialization," one of four theoretical explanations reviewed in their discussion of high black crime rates. They ultimately conclude that "tenuous and incomplete evidence" underlies each of the four theories. Thus, they have no definitive explanation for high black crime rates. James Q. Wilson and Richard J. Herrnstein, *Crime and Human Nature* (New York: Free Press, 1985), 476, 486.

37   Daniel Patrick Moynihan, *The Moynihan Report: The Negro Family: The Case for National Action* (Office of Policy Planning and Research, United States Department of Labor, 1965).

38   Kenneth B. Clark, *Dark Ghetto: Dilemmas of Social Power*, 2nd ed. (Middletown, CT: Wesleyan University Press, 1989, 1965), 106.

39   Moynihan, *Moynihan Report*, 30, italics in original.

40   Moynihan, 37–40, 47.

41   Hinton, *From the War on Poverty*, 99.

42   Clark, *Dark Ghetto*, 81.

43   Clark, 81.

44   Daniel Patrick Moynihan, memorandum to President Richard Nixon, January 16, 1970. See, e.g., "Opinion: Moynihan's Memo Fever," *Time*, March 23, 1970, 15.

45   Hinton, *From the War on Poverty*, 181.

46   Moynihan, memorandum to President Richard Nixon.

47   Shahid M. Shahidullah, *Crime Policy in America: Laws, Institutions, and Programs*, 2nd ed. (Lanham, MD: University Press of America, 2016), 17.

48   Comprehensive Drug Abuse Prevention and Control Act, Pub. L. No. 91-513, 84 Stat. 1236 (Oct. 27, 1970).

49   Fortner, *Black Silent Majority*; Forman, *Locking Up Our Own*.

50   Hinton, *From the War on Poverty*, 22.

51   Hinton, 24.

52   Hinton, 24.

53   The UCR is estimated to report overall about half the crime accounted for by the national victims' survey (NCVS), although there are differences depending on the type of crime involved. Robert M. O'Brien, David Shichor, and David L. Decker, "An Empirical Comparison of the Validity of UCR and NCS Crime Rates" *Sociological Quarterly* 21, no. 3 (1980): 391–401.

54   Hinton, *From the War on Poverty*, 24.

55   Matthew Friedman and James Cullen, "JustFacts: What Clearance Rates Say about Disparities in Crime and Prosecution," Brennan Center of Justice (blog), September 30, 2016, https://www.brennancenter.org/blog/what-clearance-rates-say-about-disparities-crime-and-prosecution-0; James P. Levine, "Clearance Rates," *Encyclopedia of Law Enforcement*, Larry Sullivan and Marie Rosen, eds. (Thousand Oaks, CA: Sage Publications, 2004), 67–69.

56   Latzer, *The Rise and Fall of Violent Crime in America*, 129–30 (see chap. 6, n. 19).

57   Hinton, *From the War on Poverty*, 24.

58   In 2016, blacks were 30 percent of those arrested for forgery, counterfeiting, fraud, and embezzlement, though they were around 12.5 percent of the population. FBI, *Uniform Crime Reports 2016*, table 21A. In 2018, blacks were 24 percent of the state and federal prisoners serving sentences for these same crimes. U.S. Department of Justice, Bureau of Justice Statistics, *Prisoners in 2019*, tables 14, 16 (see intro, n. 1).

59   Latzer, *The Rise and Fall of Violent Crime in America*, 143 (see chap. 6, n. 19).

60   Hinton, *From the War on Poverty*, 24-5. It is noteworthy that crime is usually overwhelmingly intramural, so the vast majority of African American offenders victimize other persons of color. In 2018, the offender was of the same race as the victim in 70 percent of violent incidents involving black victims. U.S. Department of Justice, Bureau of Justice Statistics, *Criminal Victimization, 2018* (2019), 1.

CHAPTER 10: THE MYTH OF OVERPUNISHMENT

1   U.S. Department of Justice Bureau of Justice Statistics, *Prisoners in 2019*, 1 (see intro., n. 1).

2   *Time* magazine published a Brennan Center proposal to reduce imprisonment by 39 percent. Lauren-Brooke Eisen and Inimai Chettiar, "39% of Prisoners Should Not Be in Prison," *Time*, December 9, 2016, https://time.com/4596081/incarceration-report/. The American Civil Liberties Union trumped this with a 50 percent proposal for prisons and jails. Taylor Pendergrass, "We Can Cut Mass Incarceration by 50 Percent,"ACLU blog, July 12, 2019, https://www.aclu.org/blog/smart-justice/mass-incarceration/we-can-cut-mass-incarceration-50-percent.

3   Rachel Kushner, "Is Prison Necessary?," *New York Times Magazine,* April 21, 2019, https://www.nytimes.com/2019/04/17/magazine/prison-abolition-ruth-wilson-gilmore.html. The *Harvard Law Review* has given intellectual respectability to the abolition drive, devoting an entire volume to the issue. Vol. 132, 2019.

4   In 2019, there were 1,430,800 state and federal prisoners in the United States, and 878,900 parolees. U.S. Department of Justice, Bureau of Justice Statistics, *Correctional Populations in the United States, 2019 – Statistical Tables* (2021), table 1. In the same year, the adult population of the United States, ages 18 and above, was 250,564,000. U.S. Census Bureau, "Age and Sex Composition in the United States: 2019," table 1, https://www.census.gov/data/tables/2019/demo/age-and-sex/2019-age-sex-composition.

html. Regarding recidivism: state prisoners released in 2005 had a per-inmate average of 10.6 arrests and 4.9 convictions prior to their release. U.S. Department of Justice, Bureau of Justice Statistics, *Recidivism of Prisoners Released in 30 States in 2005: Patterns from 2005 to 2010* (2014), table 5. Eighty-three percent were rearrested during the nine year period following release, for a total of 1,994,000 arrests. U.S. Department of Justice, Bureau of Justice Statistics, *2018 Update on Prisoner Recidivism*, 1 (see chap. 4, n. 9).

5   Natalie N. Martinez, YongJei Lee, John E. Eck, and SooHyun O, "Ravenous Wolves Revisited: A Systematic Review of Offending Concentration," *Crime Science* 6(10) (2017), https://crimesciencejournal. biomedcentral.com/articles/10.1186/s40163-017-0072-2. This meta-analysis of 42 studies confirmed the well-established proposition that crime is highly concentrated in a small proportion of the population.

6   Murder includes non-negligent manslaughter. Victims: U.S. Department of Justice, Bureau of Justice Statistics, *Criminal Victimization, 2019* (2020), table 1 (see intro., n. 3). Known Crimes: FBI, *Uniform Crime Reports 2019*, table 1 (see intro., n. 4). Arrests: FBI, Crime Data Explorer, Arrest Data, https:// crime-data-explorer.app.cloud.gov/pages/explorer/crime/arrest. Prison Admissions: *National Corrections Reporting Program, 1991-2019: Selected Variables*, ICPSR 38048, July 15, 2021, https://www.icpsr.umich. edu/web/NACJD/studies/38048/variables#.

7   U.S. Department of Justice, Bureau of Justice Statistics, *Prisoners in 2019*, table 13.

8   U.S. Department of Justice, Bureau of Justice Statistics, *Multistate Criminal History Patterns of Prisoners Released in 30 States* (2015), app tables 1, 3; U.S. Department of Justice, Bureau of Justice Statistics, *2018 Update on Prisoner Recidivism* (see chap. 4, n. 9).

9   Marie Gottschalk, *Caught: The Prison State and the Lockdown of American Politics* (Princeton: Princeton University Press, 2016), 166.

10   In 2000, 19.6 percent of state prisoners who were released had completed their terms. U.S. Department of Justice, Bureau of Justice Statistics, "Reentry Trends in the U.S." (2004), https://www.bjs.gov/ content/pub/pdf/reentry.pdf.

11   U.S. Department of Justice, *Felony Sentences in State Courts,* table 1.2 (see intro., n. 2).

12   U.S. Department of Justice, Bureau of Justice Statistics, *Time Served in State Prison, 2016* (2018), table 1. For violent crimes, as one would expect, the time served is greater: 4.7 years (mean), and 2.4 years (median). U.S. Department of Justice, Bureau of Justice Statistics, *Time Served in State Prison, 2016*, table 1.

13   U.S. Department of Justice, Bureau of Justice Statistics, *Time Served in State Prison, 2016*, table 1. Murder includes non-negligent manslaughter. By definition, half of all time-served amounts are higher than the median, and half are lower. The median is preferred to the mean or average when the latter is skewed by high or low outliers, such as unusually long or short sentences. Such outliers may make the average seem higher (or lower) than warranted.

14   Cahalan, *Historical Corrections Statistics in the United States*, table 3-25 (see chap. 4, n. 32).

15   Cahalan, table 3-25. See also the following reports from the U.S. Department of Justice, Bureau of Justice Statistics: *Prison Admissions and Releases, 1981* (1984), tables 11, 12; *Prison Admissions and Releases, 1982* (1985), 1; *Report to the Nation on Crime and Justice*, 2nd ed. (1988), 100; *Time Served in Prison and on Parole, 1984* (1987), table 3; *National Corrections Reporting Program, 1986* (1991), 24, table 2–3; *National Corrections Reporting Program, 1987* (1992), table 2–3; *Prisons and Prisoners in the United States* (1992), 19; *National Corrections Reporting Program, 1989* (1992), table 2–3; *National Corrections Reporting Program, 1990* (1993), table 2–3; *National Corrections Reporting Program, 1991* (1994), table 2–3; *National Corrections Reporting Program*, 1992 (1994), table 2–4; *National Corrections Reporting Program* (annual reports, 1995–2012); *Prisoners in 2013* (2014), table 17; *Time Served in State Prison, 2016*, table 1.

16   U.S. Department of Justice, Bureau of Justice Statistics, *Prisoners in 2019*, 1 (see intro., n. 1). Europe's 2018 rate was 102.5 per 100,000. Of the twenty-seven European prison systems covered, Russia (418 per 100,000) and the east European countries had the highest rates; the Scandinavian countries (e.g., Sweden, 57; Denmark, 63) had the lowest. Council of Europe, Prisons and Community Sanctions and Measures, https://www.coe.int/en/web/prison/. Canada's 2017/18 rate was 131 per 100,000, 30 percent of the U.S. rate. Statistics Canada, https://www150.statcan.gc.ca/n1/pub/85-002-x/2019001/article/00010/tbl/tbl01-eng.htm.

17   Alfred Blumstein, Michael Tonry, and Asheley Van Ness, "Cross-National Measures of Punitiveness," *Crime and Justice* 33 (2005): 347–76, table 13.

18   Latzer, *The Rise and Fall of Violent Crime in America*, 110 (see chap. 6, n. 19). For crimes cleared by arrest, see FBI, *Crime in the United States: Uniform Crime Reports—1960* (1961), 2, 13; FBI, *Crime in the United States: Uniform Crime Reports—1990* (1990), table 20. For prison admissions, see Cahalan, *Historical Corrections Statistics in the United States*, table 3-8 (see chap. 4, n. 32); U.S. Department of Justice, Bureau of Justice Statistics, *Prisoners in 2012* (2013), table 1.

19   U.S. Department of Justice, Bureau of Justice Statistics, *2018 Update on Prisoner Recidivism*, 1 (see chap. 4, n. 9); U.S. Department of Justice, Bureau of Justice Statistics, *Recidivism of Prisoners Released in 30 States in 2005: Patterns from 2005 to 2010* (2014), table 5; U.S. Department of Justice, Bureau of Justice Statistics, *Recidivism of Prisoners Released in 1994* (2002), 1; U.S. Department of Justice, Bureau of Justice Statistics, *Recidivism of Prisoners Released in 1983* (1989), table 3.

20   U.S. Department of Justice, Bureau of Justice Statistics, *Prisoners in 2019*, table 8 (see intro., n. 1). This annual figure seems to have been typical. See, e.g., U.S. Department of Justice, Bureau of Justice Statistics, *Prisoners in 2014* (2015), table 7, reporting 164,225 parole violators returned to prison in 2014. But it substantially undercounts probationers and parolees who violate the terms of release and are incarcerated in jails as well as prisons. In 2018 that figure totaled 406,006. U.S. Department of Justice, Bureau of Justice Statistics, *Probation and Parole in the United States, 2017–2018* (2020), app tables 3, 7.

21   A Pew study found that 43.3 percent of prisoners released in forty-one states in 2004 were returned to their cells within three years. Roughly half of these (21 percent) were for technical violations and half (22.3 percent) for new crimes. Pew Center on the States, *State of Recidivism: The Revolving Door of America's Prisons* (Washington, DC: 2011).

22   A study of convictions in large urban counties found that approximately half of violent offenders with no prior convictions were sentenced to prison, whereas around 70 percent of those with multiple priors received prison sentences. Among nonviolent offenders with no priors, around one-quarter were imprisoned, but approximately 55 percent of those with multiple prior felonies were sent to prison. U.S. Bureau of Justice Statistics, *Felony Defendants in Large Urban Counties, 2009 – Statistical Tables* (2013), 32.

23   Ewing v. California, 538 U.S. 11, 123 S. Ct. 1179, 155 L. Ed. 2d 108 (2003). Ewing stole three golf clubs priced at $399 apiece, but his long criminal record, including three burglaries and a robbery at knifepoint, earned him a life sentence with parole eligibility after twenty-five years under California's Three Strikes law. The Supreme Court upheld the law by a 5 to 4 vote. In 2012, California's electorate approved a modification of the three-strikes law barring 25-to-life sentences for offenders whose third strikes were relatively minor.

24   California's 1994 law was designed "to ensure longer prison sentences and greater punishment for those who commit a felony and have been previously convicted of serious and/or violent felony offenses." Cal. Penal Code Ann. §667(b) (1999). The law was modified in 2012 as a result of Proposition 36, enacted as Cal. Penal Code Ann. §1170.126 (2017). The modification limits automatic life sentences to those whose third conviction was for a violent crime or a serious nonviolent felony, and permits reduction of previously imposed life imprisonment for those who would no longer qualify for such a sentence under the amended law. Proposition 36 was widely approved by 69 percent of the voters. James P. Levine, "De-

constructing the Politics of Three-Strikes Sentencing Reforms in California," *ACJS Today* 39, no. 2 (2014): 29–33. One reason for the approval was the imposition of striker sentences on defendants whose crimes of conviction were minor or nonserious, which occurred with 56 percent of those imprisoned under the law. Though this may seem unjust, second and third strikers had committed more crimes than other inmates: an average of three prior felonies (two of which were serious or violent) versus an average of one prior for all other inmates. Brian Brown and Greg Jolivette (the Legislative Analyst's Office), "A Primer: Three Strikes: The Impact after More Than a Decade," https://lao.ca.gov/2005/3_Strikes/3_strikes_102005.htm.

25   Brown and Jolivette, "A Primer: Three Strikes."

26   Paolo Buonanno et al., "Crime in Europe and the United States: Dissecting the 'Reversal of Misfortunes'," *Economic Policy* 26, no. 67 (2011): 352. Europe in this study included Austria, France, Germany, Italy, the Netherlands, Spain, and the UK.

27   Buonanno et al., 352.

28   Ian O'Donnell, Eric B. Baumer, and Nicola Hughes, "Recidivism in the Republic of Ireland," *Criminology and Criminal Justice* 8, no. 2 (2008): 123–46. While the Pew study, *State of Recidivism (see note 20, above)*, found a 43 percent reimprisonment rate in the U.S., other studies found rates as high as 51 percent and 52 percent. O'Donnell, Baumer, and Hughes, table 2. Eighty-three percent of released prisoners are rearrested in the United States, but rearrest rates are higher than reconviction or reimprisonment rates. U.S. Department of Justice, Bureau of Justice Statistics, *2018 Update on Prisoner Recidivism*, 1 (see chap. 4, n. 9). Recidivism measures across countries are inconsistent, but the most common measure is reconviction two years after release from prison. Only three comparable countries, Denmark, Sweden, and New Zealand, have two-year reconviction rates as high as 60 percent, the United States rate. Denis Yukhnenko, Shivpriya Sridhar, and Seena Fazel, "A Systematic Review of Criminal Recidivism Rates Worldwide: 3-Year Update," *Wellcome Open Research* 4, no. 28 (2020), https://doi.org/10.12688/wellcomeopenres.14970.3.

29   Compare New York Penal Law §160.15 (robbery first degree) and §160.05 (robbery third degree).

30   Thomas B. Marvell and Carlisle E. Moody, "The Impact of Enhanced Prison Terms for Felonies Committed with Guns," *Criminology* 33, no. 2 (1995): 259–60. This study found that gun sentence enhancement laws did not increase prison admissions or prison populations, but there were no findings on sentences or time served.

31   Nils Duquet and Maarten Van Alstein, *Firearms and Violent Deaths in Europe: An Exploratory Analysis of the Linkages Between Gun Ownership, Firearms Legislation and Violent Death* (Brussels: Flemish Peace Institute, 2015), 25; Centers for Disease Control and Prevention, National Vital Statistics System, 2001–2012.

32   FBI, *Crime in the United States 2019*, expanded homicide data table 7 (73.7 percent of homicides were committed with firearms, 11.4 percent by knives or other cutting instruments).

33   United States data from Gun Violence Archive, https://www.gunviolencearchive.org/. European data from Wikipedia, https://en.wikipedia.org/wiki/Category:Mass_shootings_in_Europe_by_year.

34   U.S. Department of Justice, Bureau of Justice Statistics, *Prisoners in 2019*, table 13 (see intro., n. 1). Arrests for murder and manslaughter comprise 2.2 percent of violent index crime arrests. FBI, *Crime in the United States 2019*, table 29.

35   U.S. Department of Justice, Bureau of Justice Statistics, *Jail Inmates in 2019* (see intro., n. 1).

36   U.S. Department of Justice, Bureau of Justice Statistics, *Jail Inmates in 2019*.

37   The total state and federal prison population at year-end 2019 was 1,430,800. U.S. Department of Justice, Bureau of Justice Statistics, *Prisoners in 2019* (see intro., n. 1). The average time served in state prison for inmates released in 2018 was 2.7 years, or 985.5 days. U.S. Department of Justice, Bureau of Justice Statistics, *Time Served in State Prison, 2018* (see intro., n. 6).

38   U.S. Department of Justice, Bureau of Justice Statistics, *Jail Inmates in 2019* (see intro., n. 1). In 2019, inmates spent an average of twenty-six days in jail. This figure includes inmates released within a day or two of arrest as well as inmates held longer because they were unable to make bail, were convicted and awaiting sentence, or were serving a sentence.

39   United States v. Salerno, 481 U.S. 739 (1987).

40   Barry Latzer, "New York's Bad Bail-Reform Law," *National Review*, January 7, 2020, https://www.nationalreview.com/2020/01/new-york-state-bail-reform-law-wont-work/. NYPD chief Dermot Shea also condemned the law. Dermot Shea, "New York's New Bail Laws Harm Public Safety," *New York Times*, January 23, 2020, https://www.nytimes.com/2020/01/23/opinion/shea-nypd-bail-reform.html.

41   Paul G. Cassell and Richard Fowles, "Does Bail Reform Increase Crime? An Empirical Assessment of the Public Safety Implications of Bail Reform in Cook County, Illinois," University of Utah College of Law Research Paper no. 349, February 19, 2020, https://papers.ssrn.com/sol3/papers.cfm?abstract_id=3541091.

42   For New York, see Department of Corrections and Community Supervision Fact Sheet, April 1, 2021, https://doccs.ny.gov/system/files/documents/2021/04/doccs-fact-sheet-april-2021_1.pdf. For Norway, see the Institute for Crime and Justice Policy Research's World Prison Brief, https://www.prisonstudies.org/sites/default/files/resources/downloads/wppl_12.pdf (1918 data).

43   Researchers interested in cross-national comparisons on criminal justice issues should start with Jim Lynch's astute article: James P. Lynch, "Comparison of Prison Use in England, Canada, West Germany, and the United States: A Limited Test of the Punitive Hypothesis," *Journal of Criminal Law & Criminology* 79 (1988–1989): 180–217.

CHAPTER 11: DECARCERATION?

1   John Gage, "AOC Floats 'Prison Abolition' to End 'American Apartheid'," *Washington Examiner*, October 7, 2019, https://www.washingtonexaminer.com/news/american-apartheid-aoc-floats-prison-abolition.
2   The Brennan Center favors a 39 percent reduction in prison inmates, whereas the American Civil Liberties Union endorsed a 50 percent cut in prison and jail populations. Eisen and Chettiar, "39% of Prisoners Should Not Be in Prison"; Pendergrass, "We Can Cut Mass Incarceration by 50 Percent (see chap. 10, n. 2, for both citations),
3   Jeremy Travis, former president of John Jay College of Criminal Justice, says that "abolition has become a rallying cry for the progressive wing of the justice reform movement" and there is "lots of energy" behind it. Bill Keller, "What Do Abolitionists Really Want?," The Marshall Project, June 13, 2019, https://www.themarshallproject.org/2019/06/13/what-do-abolitionists-really-want; "Black Lives Matter Co-Founder Patrisse Cullors Talks Prison Abolition, Therapy as Reparations, and Teaming Up with Angela Davis and Yara Shahidi," *Teen Vogue*, February 22, 2019, https://www.teenvogue.com/story/black-lives-matter-patrisse-cullors-interview-prison-abolition-angela-davis-yara-shahidi; John Washington, "What Is Prison Abolition?," *Nation*, July 21, 2018, https://www.thenation.com/article/archive/what-is-prison-abolition/. For full-length analyses linking abolition to much broader leftist agendas, see Angela Y. Davis, *Abolition Democracy: Beyond Empire, Prisons, and Torture* (New York: Seven Stories Press, 2005), 103; and Allegra M. McLeod, "Envisioning Abolition Democracy," *Harvard Law Review* 132 (2019): 1619.
4   See my work on the history of violent crime in the United States. Latzer, *The Roots of Violent Crime in America* (see chap. 4, n. 31); and Latzer, *The Rise and Fall of Violent Crime in America* (see chap. 6, n. 19). As I demonstrate, neither poverty nor racism nor both factors combined sufficiently explain high violent crime rates, whereas group subcultures of violence are an overlooked major factor.

5   See, e.g., Michelle Alexander, "Reckoning with Justice," *New York Times*, March 3, 2019, https://www.nytimes.com/2019/03/03/opinion/violence-criminal-justice.html.

6   U.S. Department of Justice, Bureau of Justice Statistics, *2018 Update on Prisoner Recidivism* (see chap. 4, n. 9).

7   James Austin and Lauren-Brooke Eisen, *How Many Americans Are Unnecessarily Incarcerated?* (New York: Brennan Center for Justice, 2016), https://www.brennancenter.org/sites/default/files/2019-08/Report_Unnecessarily_Incarcerated_0.pdf, 7.

8   Austin and Eisen, 40.

9   Austin and Eisen, 9, 32.

10   Austin and Eisen, 21–22.

11   Austin and Eisen, 3.

12   United States Sentencing Commission, *Length of Incarceration and Recidivism* (2020), 4, https://www.ussc.gov/sites/default/files/pdf/research-and-publications/research-publications/2020/20200429_Recidivism-SentLength.pdf. See also Elizabeth Berger and Kent S. Scheidegger, *Sentence Length and Recidivism: A Review of the Research* (2021), http://mail.cjlf.org/publications/papers/SentenceRecidivism.pdf, finding "no substantial evidence" that longer sentences have a criminogenic effect.

13   U.S. Department of Justice, Bureau of Justice Statistics, *Recidivism of Prisoners Released in 30 States in 2005: Patterns from 2005 to 2010* (2014), table 16. The report defines recidivism as reincarceration in jail or prison within three years of release provided there is a new sentence for the crime. This occurs with 36.2 percent of released prisoners. The better benchmark is all those returned to prison with a parole or probation revocation *or* a new sentence, which totals 49.7 percent of released offenders. Often parolees or probationers commit new crimes and are reincarcerated for violating their release requirements rather than being charged with a new offense. They should be counted as recidivists.

14   Austin and Eisen, *How Many Americans Are Unnecessarily Incarcerated?*, 42. We have a serious mental health problem among inmates in criminal justice system facilities. A federal study once found that 56 percent of the incarcerated reported a mental health disorder. U.S. Dept of Justice, Bureau of Justice Statistics, *Mental Health Problems of Prison and Jail Inmates* (2006). But it probably would require the reopening of psychiatric hospitals to deal with this issue in a meaningful way.

15   A meta-analysis of 154 studies of adult and juvenile drug courts and special DWI courts found a 38 percent recidivism rate (42 percent for the juvenile court) after one year in most of the studies. Ojmarrh Mitchell et al., "Assessing the Effectiveness of Drug Courts on Recidivism: A Meta-Analytic Review of Traditional and Non-Traditional Drug Courts," *Journal of Criminal Justice* 40, no. 1 (2012): 60–71.

16   David A. Boyum, Jonathan P. Caulkins, and Mark A. R. Kleiman, "Drugs, Crime, and Public Policy," in *Crime and Public Policy*, ed. James Q. Wilson and Joan Petersilia (New York: Oxford University Press, 2011), 385.

17   Sixty-two percent of property offenders are returned to prison in three years. That's the highest return rate for any crime category. U.S. Department of Justice, Bureau of Justice Statistics, *Recidivism of Prisoners Released in 30 States in 2005*, table 16.

18   U.S. Department of Justice, Bureau of Justice Statistics, *Prisoners in 2019*, table 14 (see intro., n. 1).

19   Cassia Spohn, *How Do Judges Decide: The Search for Fairness and Justice in Punishment*, 2nd ed. (Thousand Oaks, CA: Sage, 2009), 184, emphasis added.

20   Latzer, *The Rise and Fall of Violent Crime in America*, 259–60 (see chap. 6, n. 19). Nowadays, we don't associate Irish Americans or Italian Americans with high violent crime rates, but their level of crime involvement was great in the late nineteenth and early twentieth centuries. Their movement to the middle class seems to have made all the difference. See Latzer, *The Roots of Violent Crime in America*, xiv, and passim.

CHAPTER 12: E-CARCERATION

1   Travis C. Pratt, et al., "The Empirical Status of Deterrence Theory: A Meta-Analysis," in *Taking Stock: The Status of Criminological Theory*, ed. Francis T. Cullen, John Wright, and Kristie Blevins (London: Routledge, 2017), 367-395.

2   Latzer, *The Rise and Fall of Violent Crime in America*, 252–56 (see chap. 6, n. 19).

3   David Farabee, *Rethinking Rehabilitation: Why Can't We Reform Our Criminals?* (Washington, DC: AEI Press, 2005). For a critique, see Francis T. Cullen et al., "Nothing Works Revisited: Deconstructing Farabee's *Rethinking Rehabilitation*," *Victims & Offenders* 4, no. 2 (2009): 101–23, https://doi.org/10.1080/15564880802612565.

4   The Pew Charitable Trusts, "Use of Electronic Offender-Tracking Devices Expands Sharply," September 7, 2016, http://www.pewtrusts.org/en/research-and-analysis/issue-briefs/2016/09/use-of-electronic-offender-tracking-devices-expands-sharply.

5   A recent United States Supreme Court case, Carpenter v. United States, 585 U.S. __, 138 S. Ct. 2206, 201 L. Ed. 2d 507 (2018), held, by a 5-4 vote, that police need a warrant to obtain cell phone-generated location information from phone service providers. However, this ruling did not discuss probationers and parolees, who have diminished Fourth Amendment rights. United States v. Knight, 534 U.S. 112 (2001) (no warrant required to search probationer's home with reasonable suspicion). Samson v. California, 547 U.S. 843, 126 S. Ct. 2193, 165 L. Ed. 2d 250 (2006) (upholding search of parolee without reasonable suspicion).

6   William Bales et al., *A Quantitative and Qualitative Assessment of Electronic Monitoring* (Florida State University, 2010), 150, https://www.ncjrs.gov/pdffiles1/nij/grants/230530.pdf.

7   Jenny Williams and Don Weatherburn, "Can Electronic Monitoring Reduce Reoffending?," *Review of Economics and Statistics* (August 10, 2020): 1–46, https://doi.org/10.1162/rest_a_00954 (Australian study. Compared with prison, electronic monitoring is estimated to reduce the probability of reoffending by 22 percentage points five years after sentencing and by 11 percentage points ten years after sentencing, with the cumulative number of offenses reduced by 45 percent ten years after sentencing); Martin Killias et al., "Community Service versus Electronic Monitoring—What Works Better? Results of a Randomized Trial," *British Journal of Criminology* 50, no. 6 (2010): 1155–70 (controlled study in Switzerland); Efrat Shoham, Shirley Yehosha-Stern, and Rotem Efodi, "Recidivism Among Licenced Released Prisoners Who Participated in the EM Program in Israel," *International Journal of Offender Therapy and Comparative Criminology* 59 (2015): 913–29 (Israeli study, 2007–2009, 155 subjects); Synøve N. Andersen and Kjetil Telle, *Electronic Monitoring and Recidivism: Quasi-Experimental Evidence from Norway*, discussion paper no. 844, Statistics Norway, Research Department, Oslo (2016), https://www.econstor.eu/bitstream/10419/192826/1/dp844.pdf.

8   Anaïs Henneguelle, Benjamin Monnery, and Annie Kensey, "Better at Home than in Prison? The Effects of Electronic Monitoring on Recidivism in France," *Journal of Law and Economics* 59, no. 3 (2016): 629–67.

9   Electronic Frontier Foundation, "Electronic Monitoring; Street-Level Surveillance," accessed May 27, 2021, https://www.eff.org/pages/electronic-monitoring.

10   Grady v. North Carolina, 575 U.S. __, 135 S. Ct. 1368, 1370 (2015). On remand, the North Carolina Supreme Court, by a 4-2 vote, held that a statute requiring lifelong tracking of a recidivist sex offender who had served his time and wasn't on probation or parole was unconstitutional. State v. Grady, 831 S.E.2d 542 (N.C. 2019).

11   *Samson*, 547 U.S. at 853.

12   *Samson*, 547 U.S. 843 (upholding the search of a parolee without reasonable suspicion); United States v. Knight, 534 U.S. 112 (2001) (no warrant required to search probationer's home with reasonable suspicion).

13   Commonwealth v. Cory, 454 Mass. 559, 911 N.E.2d 187 (2009); Commonwealth v. Feliz, 481 Mass. 689, 119 N.E.3d 700 (2019). Because the decision in the *Feliz* case was based on the state constitution, not the U.S. Constitution, it cannot be reversed by the United States Supreme Court.

14   U.S. Department of Justice, Bureau of Justice Statistics, *Recidivism of Sex Offenders Released from State Prison: A 9-Year Follow-Up (2005-14)* (2019).

15   *Cory*, 454 Mass. at 570.

16   Balleau v. Wall, 811 F.3d 929 (7th Cir. 2016). .

17   In Kansas v. Hendricks, 521 U.S. 346, 117 S. Ct. 2072 138 L. Ed. 2d 501 (1997), the Supreme Court upheld the indefinite civil commitment of a prisoner convicted of a sex offense who had served his sentence, but whom the state deemed dangerous due to a mental abnormality.

18   Ex post facto laws impose punishments retroactively. They violate Article I, section 9 of the U.S. Constitution (applicable to the federal government), and Article I, section 10 (applicable to the states).

19   *Balleau*, 811 F.3d at 932–33.

20   *Balleau*, 811 F.3d at 935.

21   *Balleau*, 811 F.3d at 936.

22   *Balleau*, 811 F.3d at 937.

23   A good illustration is Justice David H. Souter, appointed to the High Court by President George H. W. Bush in 1990 with the expectation that he would be a judicial conservative. At first, he was a "swing vote," but in his last years on the bench (he retired in 2009), he regularly voted with the liberal wing of the court. Ross Douthat, "David Souter Killed the Filibuster," *New York Times*, April 12, 2017.

24   Mirko Bagaric, Dan Hunter, and Gabrielle Wolf, "Technological Incarceration and the End of the Prison Crisis," *Journal of Criminal Law & Criminology* 108 (2018): 73-135.

25   Bagaric, Hunter, and Wolf, 103.

26   Bagaric, Hunter, and Wolf, 104.

27   Bagaric, Hunter, and Wolf, 105.

28   Virender Singha, Swati Singha, and Pooja Gupta, "Real-Time Anomaly Recognition Through CCTV Using Neural Networks," *Procedia Computer Science* 173 (2020): 254–63 (paper presented at International Conference on Smart Sustainable Intelligent Computing).

29   Bagaric, Hunter, and Wolf, "Technological Incarceration and the End of the Prison Crisis," 109.

30   Bagaric, Hunter, and Wolf, 110.

31   Bagaric, Hunter, and Wolf, 79.

32   U.S. Department of Justice, Bureau of Justice Statistics, *Prisoners in 2019* (see intro., n. 1).

33   U.S. Department of Justice, Bureau of Justice Statistics, *Probation and Parole in the United States, 2017–2018* (2020), app. table 7.

34   U.S. Department of Justice, Bureau of Justice Statistics, *2018 Update on Prisoner Recidivism*, 1 (see chap. 4, n. 9).

35   In 2018, defendants sentenced to state prison for all offenses were expected to serve 44.4 percent of an average 6.7-year sentence, that is, three years behind bars, three years and nine months on parole or similar release procedure. For violent crimes, the expectation was that 52.5 percent of a 10.8 year sentence would be served, or 5.7 years in prison, 5.2 years on parole or similar release procedure. U.S. Department of Justice, Bureau of Justice Statistics, *Time Served in State Prison, 2018*, table 3 (see intro., n. 6).

36   U.S. Department of Justice, Bureau of Justice Statistics, *Probation and Parole in the United States, 2017–2018* (2020), app. table 3. The unincarcerated but unsuccessful probationers absconded, had warrants, or failed for other reasons.

37   *Samson*, 547 U.S. 843.

NAME INDEX

SUBJECT INDEX

solitary confinement, 57–58.
US Supreme Court decisions on prisoners' rights, 66–68.
low-level offences, 96–97, 169n7.
eliminating imprisonment for, 94, 128–29, 130, 131.
recidivism rates for, 130.
restorative justice and, 126.

mass incarceration, xi, xiii, 73, 86, 90, 94, 153, 169n19, 172n2, 176n3. *See also* decarceration.
effects on crime rate, 83.
drug offenders and rates of, 87, 88–92, 108, 131.
incorrect definition of, 88.
restorative justice (failure to end), 127–28.
jails and, 120–21.
myth of, xi, 123.
racial imbalance and, 90–91, 128, 130–31.
methods of capital punishment
electrocution, 50,
firing squad, 51.
hanging, 49–50.
lethal gas, 50–51.
lethal injection, 51.

original sin, 10.
overpunishment (myth of), 105–24.
current rates of incarceration, 105, 106, 109–12.
effects of gun crime, 118–20.
effects of recidivism, 115–17.
effects of sentence length, 113–14.
homicide rates, 117–18.
jails, effect on incarceration rates, 120–21.
length of sentences vs time served, 105.
reasons for incarceration, 107t, 113–16.
"three strikes" law, effects of, 116–17.
US rates compared to other countries, 112–13, 117–19.

parole, 17, 27–30, 31, 36, 43, 54, 64, 67, 68, 88, 89–90, 110, 127, 133. *See also* e-carceration.
definition of, 89–90.
failure of parolees to comply with conditions of, 115.
percentage of African American parolees, 90.
percentage of offenders on, 88, 110.
public reaction to, 30.
sentences without possibility of, 53, 133.

penal farms, 26, 39, 59, 65. *See also* Parchman prison.
prior arrests of prisoners, 108, 114.
prison system, early development of in US, 9–18. *See also* Walnut Street Jail.
attitudes toward capital/corporal punishment, 9, 10, 11.
forced silence in, 15.
flogging prohibited, 16.
harsh discipline in, 14–15, 16, 17.
length of prison sentences, 17.
problems of, 16.
reform movement and, 15–16, 17–18.
rehabilitation as goal, 10, 11, 15.
social pressure viewed as cause of criminality, 10–11.
prisoners' rights movement, 109, 115.
probation, 88–90, 115, 126, 127, 132, 134, 136–37.
number of people on, 89.
rates of recidivism, 89, 115.
progressive era, prison reform during, 27–36. *See also* Elmira prison.
beginnings of, 27–28, 36.
education in prisons, 31.
eugenics in, 33–34.
evaluation of results, 32–33, 35.
homicide rates at end of, 35.
indeterminate sentencing and "good time" laws, 28–29, 31.
methods of, 28.
parole in, 28–30, 31.
physical improvements to facilities, 28.
sterilization in, 34.
stiffer sentences for recidivism, 30–31.

recidivism, xiii, 32, 62, 69, 113, 115–17, 125, 132, 140, 149, 160n9, 174n20, 175n28, 177n12–13, 177n15, 177n17, 178n7. *See also* repeat offenders.
e-carceration and, 134, 136, 139, 143.
rates for low-level crimes, 130.
rates of compared to time served, 129.
US rates compared to European, 117–18.
repeat offenders, xiii, 55, 62, 123. *See also* recidivism.
sentencing of, 30, 96, 116.
restorative justice, 126–28.